REPEAL UNEMPLOYMENT!

FOR PRESIDENT

NORMAN

THOMAS

FOR VICE-PRESIDENT

JAMES H.

MAURER

VOTE SOCIALIST

Marshall Cavendish
Benchmark
New York

REPEAL UNEMPLOYMENT!

FOR PRESIDENT

NORMAN

THOMAS

FOR VICE-PRESIDENT

JAMES H.

MAURER

VOTE SOCIALIST

socialism

THOMAS FLEMING

Marshall Cavendish Benchmark
99 White Plains Road • Tarrytown, NY
10591 • www.marshallcavendish.us
Library of Congress Cataloging-
in-Publication Data • Fleming, Thomas,
1945- • Socialism / by Thomas Fleming.
p. cm.—(Political systems of the world)
Summary: "Discusses socialism as a
political system, and details the • history of
socialist governments throughout the
world"—Provided by publisher. • Includes
bibliographical references. • ISBN-13: 978-
0-7614-2632-5 • 1. Socialism—History. 2.
Socialism. I. Title. II. Series. • HX36.F56
2007 • 320.53'1—dc22 • 2006033048

Photo research by Connie Gardner
Cover photo by The Granger Collection •
Photographs in this book are used by
permission and through the courtesty of: *The
Granger Collection*: 1, 3, 6, 8, 22; Corbis:
Alinari Archives, 16; Leonard de Selva, 27;
Archivo Iconografico, S.A., 32, back cover;
John van Hasselt/Sygma, 39; Underwood
and Underwood, 55; Bettmann, 61, 83;
Hulton Deutsch Collection, 72; Corbis, 97;
Belousov Vitaly/ITAR-TASS, 103; *Getty*:
Hulton Archives, 90; Time Life Pictures,
108; *The Image Works*: Mary Evans Picture
Library, 120–121.

Publisher: Michelle Bisson
Art Director: Anahid Hamparian
Series Designer: Sonia Chaghatzbanian
Printed in Malaysia
1 3 5 6 4 2

3764

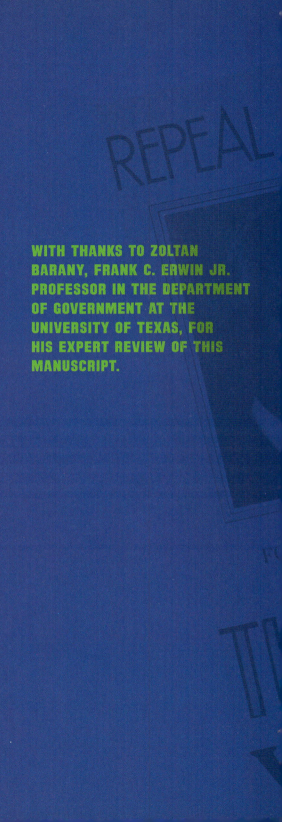

WITH THANKS TO ZOLTAN
BARANY, FRANK C. ERWIN JR.
PROFESSOR IN THE DEPARTMENT
OF GOVERNMENT AT THE
UNIVERSITY OF TEXAS, FOR
HIS EXPERT REVIEW OF THIS
MANUSCRIPT.

Contents

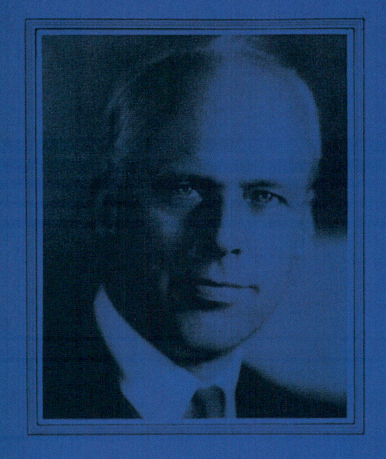

FOR PRESIDENT

NORMAN

THOMAS

FOR

MA

VOTE SOCI

MENT!

CE-PRESIDENT

MES H.

URER

LIST

socialism

REPEAL UNEMPLOYMENT!

FOR PRESIDENT

NORMAN

THOMAS

FOR VICE-PRESIDENT

JAMES H.

MAURER

VOTE SOCIALIST

An Essential Introduction ■ ■ ■

PEOPLE OFTEN THROW AROUND WORDS like *socialist* and *communist* and *liberal* as if they were meaningless insults. In fact, all these terms, though each has evolved over time, has a fairly precise meaning. Before talking about political movements and parties, we should first have an idea of what the basic words mean. This is not always easy. Socialism, for example, is a complex and ever-changing phenomenon. The term was originally applied to a political economic system with public ownership of large industries and corporations. Dozens of socialist parties came into existence in the late nineteenth and early twentieth centuries, but socialist policies also came to be adopted by liberal and conservative parties, sometimes as a means of luring working-class voters. No democratic country has ever gone completely socialist, and communist countries, which have come closest to realizing socialist theory, have been transformed by force—either by revolution, as in China and Russia, or, in most other cases, by conquest. Although there are general trends in socialist legislation and administration, there are an almost infinite variety of socialist experiments, from Cambodia's ruthless elimination of nonpeasants to the bland social democracy adopted voluntarily by the Scandinavian nations.

Socialist parties have also changed over the course of time. Many political parties that began by openly calling for public ownership of factories, mines, and utilities gradually dropped their more radical demands in favor of more general advocacy of economic fairness, wage increases, and improved health and welfare systems. By the end of the twentieth century they had adopted a wide range of new social issues, such as feminism, gay rights, and environmentalism.

The variety of socialist parties and their chameleonlike ability to adapt to changing circumstances make generalizations difficult, and to make matters worse, any general treatment of socialism runs the risk of misleading readers into imagining that socialist theory has been calmly and rationally applied as a remedy for social problems. In fact, socialist politicians can be as ambitious, greedy, and opportunistic as other politicians, and the peculiar turns taken by socialism in, say, Albania or Chile, have more to do with the character of the people and their socialist leaders than with any political theory. Despite all these contradictions, it is not too difficult to sketch out socialism's basic principles or to trace them through the twists and turns that socialist parties have made.

Many general treatments of socialism have concentrated only on Western Europe. This approach limits the focus much too narrowly and encourages the ethnocentric view that everything important happens only in such countries as France and Britain. In fact, non-Western and non-European countries have made important experiments in socialist policy. To avoid the pitfalls of overgeneralization, three countries have been singled out for concentrated attention: Germany, the country that produced the most significant socialist theorists and the first successful socialist party; the United Kingdom, because it is home to one of the oldest and most influential socialist movements in the world, and Sweden, whose family policies illustrate the social dimension of modern socialism. Significant examples will also be drawn from Titoist Yugoslavia, as a nonaligned communist state that allowed some private property and entrepreneurship, Mexico as an example of an underdeveloped and non-European country with a legacy of colonialism, and, finally, the United States, whose socialist policies have always been misleadingly described as "liberal." This variety—both in extent and type of socialist policies—should offer a more secure basis for generalized conclusions about the success or failure of socialism.

The inclusion of New Deal and Great Society programs in an introductory book on socialism may be somewhat surprising. In the

United States, unfortunately, political discourse has been complicated by the deliberate misuse of terms. Historically and still for the most part, in Europe, the words liberal, conservative, and socialist have had clear and distinct meanings. In the European tradition, liberals, often known as classical liberals and libertarians in the United States, believe (as their name suggests) in liberty. Socialists, by contrast, emphasize economic justice, the redistribution of wealth and opportunity, and state ownership or control of great economic interests.

Classical liberal movements and parties oppose all unnecessary obstacles to individual liberty, self-fulfillment, and the progress of the human race. Historically, liberals argued against monarchy (though there were liberal monarchists), traditional class structures, established churches, tariffs on trade, and even (in the case of John Stuart Mill) against restrictive moral codes and the subjugation of women. Liberals believed that the best economic results would come about in a system of free competition within the marketplace.

If liberalism's code words are liberty, progress, and competition, conservatives have spoken of the importance of religion, social stability, and traditional loyalties to the family and the nation. Although conservatism, unlike liberalism, never had a clear program or ideology, conservatives instinctively resisted change, and, until the mid-twentieth century, most conservatives were, at best, lukewarm defenders of capitalism and competition. They often agreed with the moral arguments put forward by socialists who favored assistance to the poor, and they disagreed sharply with the liberal faith in free trade. Without being nationalists, conservatives are eager to defend their nations, a fact that makes international conservative cooperation extremely difficult.

In the course of the twentieth century, conservatives in the United States, the United Kingdom, and Germany adopted much of the classical liberal economic agenda, without necessarily sacrificing all of their old commitments to family, aristocracy, and religion. Liberals, as they lost the support of the working classes, either turned conservative or adopted the parts of the socialist agenda they found compatible with their own. For example, liberals originally spoke of liberty in terms of freedom from restraint, but in the late nineteenth century some of them (such as T. H. Greene) began to speak of liberty in terms of the freedom to *do* something, such as to pursue a professional career.

These liberals concluded that the poor could only pursue their plans if they were given free education.

The changing meanings of these terms can be very confusing, seeing that American "conservatives" like Ronald Reagan or William F. Buckley Jr. are really liberals, while "liberals" like Senators Edward Kennedy and Hillary Rodham Clinton are closer to being socialists than liberals. To keep things simple, I shall use conservative and liberal in their classical senses, though when capitalized they will refer to Conservative or Liberal parties (like the British Conservative Party) and their members. Since American "liberals" do not like to be called socialists, they will usually be described as "left liberals," though when their programs coincide with those of socialist parties, the spade will have to be called a spade and not a garden fork.

In a book as brief as this one, many details and fine points have to be eliminated or glossed over. Readers who wish to understand the protean (changeable) nature of socialism will have to imitate the ancient heroes who wanted to squeeze the truth out of Proteus, the Old Man of the Sea, who could change his shape from a seal to a roaring lion to a blazing fire. If they held on long enough, the heroes could finally squeeze some useful truth out of the elusive god.

Socialist Theory Before the French Revolution

WHAT IS SOCIALISM?

SOCIALISM IS BOTH A POLITICAL THEORY and a political economic system that emphasizes the duty of society to ensure social and economic fairness and equality. In pure socialist theory, this means that society, or rather government, should own and/or control the means of production, private property, and wealth, all of which have to be used for the benefit of everyone and not simply for the benefit of a rich individual or a privileged minority. In order to secure a fair distribution of wealth and income among the members of society, socialist governments typically confiscate or closely regulate major industries, the means of transportation and communication, and utilities (such as electricity and oil). They also employ a system of taxation to transfer wealth from the more affluent classes to the less affluent and to establish systems to provide pensions (social security) and health care, either for the poor or for the entire population.

Socialism arose as a response to the liberal economic (that is, free-market/capitalist) policies adopted by most Western European countries at the beginning of the nineteenth century. According to classical liberal theory, no government, church, or inherited aristocracy should be able to place obstacles in the way of any individual's success. The market within countries should be free, and even between nations there should be minimal interference. Classical Liberals, therefore, opposed both the compulsory collection of tithes for churches and tariffs (taxes) on imported goods. They believe that the free market, without government restraint, will always be the most efficient means of distributing goods and services within a society. Any attempt to constrain the market by setting a minimum wage for labor or requiring pension plans will distort the natural relationship between buyer and seller, even where "buyer" means employer and "seller" means the employee who sells his labor. To make matters thoroughly confusing, Americans who advocate liberal policies usually describe themselves as conservatives, while the so-called liberals come closer to being socialists.

Liberals usually (though not always) support capitalism, but liberalism and capitalism must be distinguished. Capitalism, although it is often confused with theories of the free market, is actually an economic system that emphasizes capital: the money invested into a company that pays wages to its employees. Capitalism either did not exist or existed in a very rudimentary form in pre-modern societies, where peasants worked their own land, workers owned their own tools, and businessmen were small shopkeepers.

In principle, capitalism is incompatible with socialism, because capitalism presupposes private property and laws protecting property, while socialists traditionally have advocated public ownership of the great economic interests. In reality, however, capitalism and socialism have tended to merge. In countries that have nationalized large businesses, capitalist managers were often hired to run the corporations, while in countries that are officially capitalistic, large corporations cooperate closely with government agencies and often secure important benefits to themselves and to the detriment of smaller rivals. In *The Wealth of Nations*, Adam Smith, the first theorist of capitalism, noted that rival businessmen would rather work together to control, by fixing wages and prices, than compete in the marketplace. Since the beginning of the twentieth century this has usually meant a close collaboration of business and government, in capitalist as much as in socialist countries.

Although no perfectly socialist society has ever been constructed, many basic socialist principles have been adopted by modern states, whether they are officially social-democratic, communist, or capitalist. The first of these is the principle of social and economic equality, regardless of such considerations as social class or inherited wealth. Sometimes this goal is expressed (for example, in communist states), as a desire for equality of condition, that is, that all people would have more or less the same wealth and property; but it can also be expressed (as it is in liberal democratic states such as the United States) as a desire for equality of opportunity, which means that each citizen has an equal chance to succeed and grow rich. To accomplish equality of either type, vast powers must be assumed by socialist governments, which redistribute incomes through tax policies, ensure equal access to education, decent housing, and health care, and eliminate the power of the traditional upper classes.

Communism is the theory of socialism advocated by Karl Marx and modified and put into practice by N. Lenin after the Russian Revolution of 1917. Although both communists and socialists agree on government ownership of the means of production (and on most other points), there are two major differences between communism and other socialist systems. First, Marx and Lenin believed that history was dominated by class conflict, and they concluded from this that no truly communist or socialist state could come into existence except by means of a violent revolution, such as occurred in Russia and China. Although many noncommunist socialists accept the theory of class conflict, they believe in a gradual, democratic evolution toward a socialist state.

The second major difference is that socialists see the socialist state as an end in itself, the permanent social and political arrangement for modern societies, whereas in communist theory, socialism is only an intermediate stage between capitalism and the ultimate communist society in which there is no state, when, as Karl Marx put it, the state will wither away. Nonetheless, the most important difference between communists and socialists has more to do with methods than with ultimate objectives. Socialists are willing to work within a system, if only to subvert it, while communists believe they must use violent means to overthrow any existing system.

Although the collapse of the Soviet empire (in the late 1980s and early 1990s) has tended to discredit communism, socialist ideas (at

Raphael's painting, *The School of Athens* (created ca. 1509–1511), depicts a group of Greek philosophers, often very different in their philosophies, but always engaged in spirited discussion of their beliefs. Some of these philosophers' ideas are considered the underpinnings of later utopian or socialist states.

least in a moderate form) are accepted and praised, even by politicians and journalists who claim to defend the free market. In the late 1880s, when the British Liberal statesman Sir William Harcourt declared, "We are all socialists now," he may have been premature. A century later, however, his statement was an accurate, if somewhat extreme, description of all the major parties of Europe and the Americas.

To understand the practice of socialism in countries today, we should first know something about how socialist ideas developed. Although socialist and communist theories were largely the product of the nineteenth century revolutionary movements that followed the French Revolution (1789–1799), the basic idea is much older. Some of the sources include the Greek philosopher Plato, the Christian New Testament, and the utopian writings of Sir Thomas More and Tommaso Campanella. While many of these theories were pure speculation, it is important to understand that socialist theories are usually generated and almost always take hold in the popular mind during periods of crisis, when faith in traditional institutions is crumbling.

THE LEGACY OF PLATO

Plato was one of the world's most original and influential philosophers. Dissatisfied with the wars and conflicts of his native Athens, he wanted to work out a theory of justice that would apply to every city-state, not just his own. Since democratic Athens (in the fifth century BCE) had created an empire, suppressed the power of the aristocracy and middle classes, and lost an all-important war with her rival Sparta, Plato, who came from a wealthy and aristocratic background, rejected democracy and turned to Sparta as the starting point for his perfect society. Sparta was ruled by a warrior elite class, whose members were called "Equals" because they supposedly had roughly the same amount of property. The sons of these Equals were reared in common with other boys and taught to live off the land. The Spartan Equals were able to devote themselves to war and politics, because their farms were tended by a race of peasant-slaves known as Helots, who were descendants of the people the Spartans had conquered.

Many Athenian aristocrats admired the Spartans for their virtue and heroism. However, by Plato's time Spartan aristocrats were acquiring large amounts of property and money, and the virtue and incorruptibility for which they were famous was disappearing. Plato's

17

political ideal would be something like an abstract version of Sparta that could survive and preserve its egalitarian system. In *The Republic,* Plato sketches out the outline of a perfectly just society, ruled by a class of guardians who have no private property and share wives and children. The lower classes, dominated by their sensual appetites, are allowed to lead normal lives, but they have no share in the government. Women of the guardian class, however, will receive the same athletic training as men and, so far as they are able, will share in power and responsibility.

Plato's contribution to socialism is threefold: First, he established the ideal of economic and social equality; second, he proposed treating children (at least the children of Guardians) as the common property of the state; third, he contributed the idea of an elite class or party that rules the state in the common interest. All three of Plato's concepts were to enjoy a long life.

Although Plato's ideas were influenced by the traditions of early Sparta, they had little appeal to most Greeks. Greek society was deeply rooted in family and kinship, and the life of the Guardians would have seemed horrifying to most Athenians of Plato's time. Plato went to Syracuse (in Sicily) to see if his friends there would implement his ideals, but the experiment was never made, and he left Sicily a sadder and perhaps wiser man. In a later work, *Laws,* Plato did not entirely abandon his idealistic political model, but he did try to adjust it to the reality of human life. His student Aristotle, in *Ethics* and *Politics,* carefully dissected *The Republic* and showed it was both unworkable and unjust. He shrewdly pointed out that common property, in particular, was impractical, since what everyone owns will be taken care of by nobody. In environmentalism, this argument, known as "The Tragedy of the Commons," is used to show that state-owned property is more likely to be abused than privately held land. Ever since Plato's time, socialist theorists have had to wrestle with the fact that human nature may not be up to the demands put on it in an ideal society.

THE CHRISTIAN CONTRIBUTION

Plato's followers were never in a position to construct a model society. Though the Neoplatonist Plotinus did persuade a Roman emperor to build a "Platonopolis" on the Bay of Naples, the project (a model society along the lines of *The Republic*) came to nothing. By the time

Plato

Plato was born in Athens about 429 BCE and died in 347. Although a poet in his youth, he became a student of Socrates and turned exclusively to philosophy. After Socrates was condemned and executed on charges of impiety and corrupting the youth, Plato began lecturing and writing dialogues, philosophical conversations in which Socrates is usually the main character. Plato traveled more than once to Sicily and became tutor to the son of the Syracusan ruler Dionysius I and a friend of Dion, a Syracusan nobleman, who later led the resistance to the tyrant Dionysius II, Plato's former student.

In Athens, Plato taught his students in a grove of trees called the Academy. He emphasized the importance of mathematics and dialectic (a form of logic) as the foundation for all serious study. His early dialogues concentrated on the difficulty of answering questions such as "What is courage," while in his middle dialogues—often works of great literary power—he outlines a theory of ideal forms that explains the sensory world in which we live, and in his last works Plato returns to his skeptical questioning. Although his political theories in *The Republic, Laws*, and *Sophist* seem totalitarian, Plato was writing as a moralist about an ideal society rather than attempting to give a blueprint for practical reform. His dislike for democracy may have stemmed in part from the Athenian democracy's decision to execute his mentor Socrates.

of Plotinus' death (270 CE), Christianity was already winning many converts throughout the Roman world. Jesus' disciples in Jerusalem had taken his sermons on sharing and charity and used them as the basis for a society in which the members, waiting for the master's return, shared their worldly possessions and probably abstained from sexual relations. In the *Acts of the Apostles*, which describes the early days of the Christian Church, it is said that:

> Neither was there any among them that lacked: for as
> many as were possessors of lands or houses sold them,
> and brought the prices of the things that were sold, and
> laid them down at the apostles' feet: and distribution was
> made unto every man according as he had need.

The Apostles' voluntary experiment in communism, however, was short-lived and probably never extended beyond the little group in Jerusalem.

The ideals of celibacy, poverty, and communal life espoused by early Christians quickly proved to be impossible for most converts. Over the centuries a distinction emerged: ordinary people would be allowed to marry and own property, while the clergy, particularly the monastic clergy, would lead a more austere life. Under the rule of St. Benedict, monks in Western Europe took vows of poverty, chastity, and obedience; they surrendered all their possessions to the monastic community, and rich and poor lived on terms of equality. These monasteries are among the most successful socialist societies ever established.

Both Christians and Jews, although they disagreed on many things, had expectations of a Golden Age that would take place when the Messiah returned (or, in the case of Jews, came the first time). Peace and plenty would reign, and men would no longer be subject to the curse laid upon Adam: "In the sweat of thy face thou shalt eat bread." Christians had no clear or consistent conception of the Millennium (the thousand years of Christ's reign on earth), and the leaders of the Christian Church, who became increasingly alarmed by the dissensions and unrealistic expectations of millenarian thought, quietly abandoned the idea of a dawning Golden Age.

Such ideas, however, did not go away, and the leaders of one after another dissident Christian sect told their followers the end was near and called upon them to reject authority and even, in some cases, the moral law, including rules against fornication, adultery, and theft. In the later Middle Ages, such doctrines were taught by Bogomils in the Balkans and Cathars in Western Europe. In the early sixteenth century, the Protestant Thomas Münzer advocated a peasant revolution against the nobility and an equal distribution of goods. His ideas were taken up by the Anabaptists. In the German city of Münster, where they established a commonwealth, the Anabaptists, after instituting a reign of terror, practiced polygamy, free love, and communism before being suppressed in 1535. However, the suppression of the Anabaptists did not put an end to millennialist sects, which resurfaced in England during the seventeenth century.

Not all forays in Christian utopianism were so anarchic or so violent. Near the end of the twelfth century, an Italian monk and theologian, Joachim de Fiore, divided history into three periods, each dominated by one of the three persons of the Trinity. In the first age, the Age of God the Father, man lived under the Old Testament law; in the second age, the age of the Son when Christianity ruled, man lived according to grace (that is, the divine favor shown to man), but in the coming third age of the Holy Spirit, grace would be complete, hardship eliminated, and men set free to live communally as monks were supposed to live.

Joachim had great influence on late Medieval and early Renaissance thought, and he helped to inspire many thinkers and movements, both Catholic and Protestant, that denounced inequality and called for a restoration of the early Christian ideal of communal wealth and property. Christian millennarianism, by emphasizing the perfect society that was just around the corner, had a strong influence on the development of socialism. While Plato had been content to sketch out the outlines of a just society, some Christian visionaries believed that this society was predestined to emerge in the not-so-distant future.

THE FIRST UTOPIAS

The two strands of communalist inspiration, Platonism and Christianity, are woven together in the person of Sir Thomas More. More had originally planned to become a priest but found he preferred a more worldly life as a lawyer. In the reign of King Henry VIII, he rose to the top of his profession as Lord Chancellor of England (1529). More

This illustration of Thomas More's *Utopia* accompanied the 1518 edition of his work. As do other socialist theorists, More's vision of Utopia eliminated inequality and private property. Unlike most modern socialists, More was a devout Catholic.

was a sincere Christian who would be executed for his defense of the Catholic Church, but he was also a Platonist. Early on, Plato had been adopted by Christian theologians such as St. Augustine, but, although he remained the supreme philosophic influence in the Eastern Church (Orthodox), Aristotle emerged as "the philosopher" in the Catholic West. It was Aristotle who most inspired scholastic philosophers, such as Thomas Aquinas.

The fifteenth century, however, had witnessed a revival of Plato, and, while Thomas More was an excellent Latinist, he had also learned enough Greek to study Plato in his original language. More's little book *Utopia* (published in 1516) shows the influence of both Christianity and Platonism. From Plato he borrowed the idea of describing a perfect society as well as many important details, and from the Christian tradition he had acquired a burning passion for social justice and charity toward the poor. Utopia (which means something like Nowhere-land in Greek) is a tropical island described by a philosophical Portuguese traveler named Raphael Hythloday.

There are many curious features to Utopian society, including a strange custom of changing their residences (by drawing lots) every ten years. Most strikingly, More anticipates many features of nineteenth century socialist theory. The resemblance may be due less to philosophical agreement than to the fact that the sixteenth century, like the nineteenth, was a time of economic and social unrest. In sixteenth century England, the gap between rich and poor was widening, with disastrous results for the poor. More reasoned that, since desire for money is the root of all evil, a just society would strike at the root of the problem by eliminating inequality of wealth and by providing security for the sick and elderly. To maintain equality, all the adult male citizens have an agricultural property to produce food, but each man and woman must also practice a skilled trade. Utopian equality, however, is limited to the patriarchal male heads of households. Unlike Plato, More does not favor the equality of women, and his view of marriage and divorce is close to the Christian ideal.

Like all ideal societies, Utopia requires a great deal of central planning and absolute authority to make it work. Although he does provide for a police force and judicial system, More is not overly concerned with enforcement. That is probably because he knew he was not drawing up a plan for any possible human society but only sketching out a blueprint that would guide sincere people toward a more just way of life.

Utopia inspired many successors throughout the seventeenth century: Tommaso Campanella's *City of the Sun* (1602) was a theocratic world-state in which all wives and children were held in common, and Francis Bacon's *New Atlantis* combined two important utopian and socialist themes: the progress of science and the political domination of knowledge-seeking scientists. Science was also on the mind of the German Lutheran Johann Andreae in *Christianopolis*, which depicts a mystical brotherhood reminiscent of the so-called Rosicrucians, an imaginary group of dedicated seekers of truth. Scientific knowledge was also important to the Moravian founder of "Pansophia" (all-wisdom), Johann Comenius. While some early utopians emphasized scientific planning, and others mystical wisdom, none had any practical effect. However, in times of political trouble, radical ideas were taken up by small but highly militant minorities.

Revolutions rarely occur in quiet times. The English Civil War (1625–1649) was the first social and political upheaval in which speculations about human equality were turned into a political program, albeit an impractical one. The Civil War began both as a parliamentary protest against King Charles I's exercise of his royal prerogatives and as a Puritan/Presbyterian revolt against the structure and forms of the Church of England. The conflict culminated in the execution of the king and the installation of Oliver Cromwell as "Lord Protector" with far more absolute power than King Charles had ever dreamed of exercising. In the course of the fighting, however, dissident religious sects and radical political idealists clamored for attention. Some of them—the Levelers and the Diggers—had dreams of establishing a new Golden Age on earth.

The Levelers were artisans and small shopkeepers who wanted universal suffrage for freemen (though not for servants) and, though they respected property rights, they had some vague ideas about economic justice. The Diggers, who were drawn from the rural poor, were more egalitarian. Though their leading spokesman, Gerrard Winstanley, often changed his mind and issued contradictory statements, the direction of his thought is clear. He dreamed of a world of small farmers, with land enough to provide for their own families and with power enough to stand up to their oppressors, the descendants of the rich Norman barons who had (in his view)

Sir Thomas More

Born in London in 1478, More studied with Renaissance humanists (classical scholars) and became one of the most famous Latin writers of his day. As a lawyer he entered the service of a difficult master, King Henry VIII, and became Lord Chancellor, in which position he worked hard to promote the interest of the king against his rivals, including the Church. However, when Henry asked him to approve the King's divorce from his wife Katherine, More refused, preferring to be executed (in 1535) rather than to betray the Catholic Church or its view of marriage. He was declared a saint and martyr on the four-hundredth anniversary of his death. More wrote many works, in Latin and English, including a life of Richard III, but his most significant and enduring book is *Utopia*, a work that influenced the entire utopian and socialist tradition.

plundered England since 1066. His lofty ideals, he came to realize, would be difficult to implement with the ordinary run of people, and Winstanley eventually advocated a rigid system of control that would compel the lazy to work and punish those who broke the rules. Although their hopes were unfulfilled, both Levelers and Diggers left behind a trail of pamphlets that would preserve their ideas and create a myth of agrarian rebellion.

THE ENLIGHTENMENT

The "Enlightenment" or, as it was also called, "the Age of Reason," was the dominant intellectual movement of the seventeenth and eighteenth centuries. There were many currents of Enlightenment, but most of them emphasized reason and science, as opposed to tradition and religion, and many leading Enlightenment thinkers challenged the fundamental institutions of European life: Christianity, the monarchy, and the aristocracy.

Though Enlightenment thinkers (like the later classical liberals) were typically more interested in individual liberties than in social justice, much less socialism, they did contribute to a climate of opinion favorable to the development of socialist thought. The most famous French writer of the eighteenth century, François Marie Arouet de Voltaire, is a case in point. Voltaire defended monarchy, accumulated money, and lived as an aristocrat, but in his later years he defended people he regarded as the victims of oppression.

One of the most original Enlightenment thinkers was the French-Swiss writer, Jean-Jacques Rousseau. In his earliest work, *Discourse on Inequality*, Rousseau revived the ancient idea that in a state of nature men are born happy and equal, though they are oppressed by societies that impose inequality. In *The Social Contract*, Rousseau built on the familiar idea that men in a state of nature had agreed to form governments as a social contract: "Man is born free," he declared in his revolutionary first sentence, "and everywhere he is in chains." In surrendering some of their natural liberties, men would receive a system of justice and the protection of the ruler, but if a ruler became tyrannical, the people had the right to rise up in revolution to reclaim their primitive rights.

This was superficially similar to Thomas Jefferson's justification of the American Revolution in the Declaration of Independence, but

Jean-Jacques Rousseau

Jean-Jacques Rousseau preached republican virtue in the last years of the French monarchy. After his death, his disciples tried to implement his theories by force during the French Revolution.

Born in Geneva, Switzerland, in 1712, Rousseau was the son of a watchmaker. Apprenticed unsuccessfully to a lawyer and then to an engraver, he never received a formal education. In Paris during the 1740s, he contributed to the *Encyclopedia*, the vast compendium of Enlightenment learning and opinion, and in 1755 he published his first work, *Discourse on Equality*. Gaining fame from such writings as his novel *La nouvelle Heloise*, his novelistic treatise on education, *Émile*, and his most important work of political theory, *The Social Contract*, he fled France to avoid arrest and went to Switzerland, which he also left to go to Britain, where the philosopher David Hume gave him refuge. He began work on his *Confessions*. Increasingly paranoid, Rousseau denounced Hume as his persecutor, returned to France in 1767, and died in 1778. Rousseau's original mind, matched by an equally brilliant prose style, took Europe by storm. Beginning as an Enlightenment intellectual, his emphasis on personal feeling and individual expression helped to create the Romantic movement. He was the dominant intellectual influence on the French Revolution.

unlike Jefferson and the writers who influenced him (Hugo Grotius and John Locke), Rousseau's revolution was social as well as political. All legitimate power came ultimately from what he called the General Will, that is, the will of the people, which had absolute authority. Only in surrendering to the power of the General Will could each citizen truly fulfill himself. Rousseau's idea of the just state was in this way closer to the utopian and socialist ideal than it was to the Anglo-American defense of individual liberty.

Rousseau developed many ideas that would later be adopted (or discovered independently) by socialists. In the *Discourse on Political Economy*, he advocated a system of graduated taxation that exempted the poor and taxed the rich at rates proportional to their surplus wealth, that is, wealth over and above what was necessary to sustain life. In his novel *Émile*, Rousseau laid the foundations for children's rights and child-centered education. Finally, in basing political authority on the General Will and in his condemnation of Christianity, Rousseau helped to shape the image of the modern state as a power rooted in democracy but tolerating no serious rivals, whether provinces, churches, or dissident political parties.

Though he went no further than to promote the concept of virtuous republicans (ancient Spartans or modern Swiss) living in small-scale societies, Rousseau's passionate arguments and beautiful prose style encouraged many educated people of the late eighteenth century to think that social and economic equality was the natural condition of human life. There is, however, a tension in his thought that almost amounts to a contradiction. Rousseau had a very high regard for freedom, especially his own, but a society that rigorously enforced equality would leave little room for individual liberty. That would be one of the most obvious lessons of the French Revolution, but it was the hardest to remember.

2

Socialist Theory After the French Revolution

MANY OF THE ENLIGHTENMENT'S POLITICAL IDEAS crystallized in the French Revolution (1789–1799), which plunged France into a maelstrom of violence and destruction. In the name of the revolutionary trinity, "Liberty, Equality, Fraternity," the king and queen were killed and along with them a significant number of the aristocracy; churches were demolished and the clergy murdered. No one was spared on the grounds of rank, age, or sex, and the violence against nuns and aristocratic women was ugly beyond belief. The Revolution did not even spare its own children, and members of one revolutionary faction after another were condemned to the guillotine. The Revolution has been celebrated and condemned, but there can be no doubt that it is the fountainhead of the revolutions that so disturbed the nineteenth and twentieth centuries.

THE MOTHER OF ALL REVOLUTIONS

The three basic principles of the Revolution seemed simple at first, but underneath the surface there were difficulties and contradictions. Liberty was a familiar concept in Western Europe. Equality was more complicated, but equality under the law was easy enough to understand, and many practical English people and Americans even believed in political (though not economic) equality. But what in the world did the

29

revolutionaries mean by "fraternity," that is, brotherhood? Christians had called each other brothers from the beginning, but fraternity implies that all citizens are brothers, regardless of their class or religion or the area or even the country they come from. Distinctions among people will then be the ultimate evil. From here it is a small step to socialism.

The French Revolution was primarily a political and economic revolution. Estates were confiscated, the produce of rural farms was taken to feed the revolutionary army and the Paris mob, and the government undertook a plan to control wages and prices. But it was also a social, cultural, and sexual revolution. Although a proposed plan for taking children from homes of "suspects" (anyone who might possibly resent the Revolution) was never implemented, prostitution and pornography flourished in revolutionary circles.

Although socialism is primarily an economic and political theory, there is also a strong tendency in socialist thinkers (including Karl Marx and Friedrich Engels) to deny legitimacy to the institutions of marriage and family and to celebrate sexual freedom. In late eighteenth century France this tendency found expression in the writings of Pierre Choderos de Laclos, Restif de Bretonne, and the Marquis de Sade. But the most influential rebel against the rules of morality and society was already dead: Jean-Jacques Rousseau. Rousseau could write beautifully about family affections (in *Émile*), though he had abandoned his own children to public relief. His emphasis on personal sentiment as a source of moral understanding provided a shortcut that bypassed both religion and formal morality. Rousseau's distaste for abstract reasoning put him at odds with one of the main currents of the Enlightenment, but the inclination to give free reign to sexual desire was not unknown to a school of thought that saw Christian morality as the enemy.

In the years leading up to the Revolution, the Palais Royal in Paris was the nerve center of the revolutionary movement. Lawyers and intellectuals could spend the evening debating politics before going on to take part in a night of debauchery—without ever leaving the precincts of the Palais Royal. Like many a teacher, Rousseau would probably have been horrified by the uses to which his ideas were put by his libertine admirers, but he was their hero, nonetheless.

Rousseau's writings had enormous influence on the revolutionary generation. Rousseau himself thought in terms of city-states, and he was not foolish enough to think his egalitarian ideals could be enforced in a large nation such as France, but his activist disciples—revolutionary leaders like Maximilien de Robespierre, Louis de Saint-Just, and Gracchus Babeuf—were so inspired by his writings and by their mistaken ideas about ancient Sparta and Rome that they had no doubts. Each dreamed, in his own way, of a centralized nation-state that would compel its subjects to lead virtuous lives without distinctions of birth, fortune, or talent.

Robespierre and Saint-Just, although they were dominant players in the French Revolution, were content to speak in fairly general terms about the social revolution they had in mind, but on the question of tactics they were quite precise: only a reign of terror could bring about the virtuous republic they envisioned. Although we often think of terrorism as something practiced solely by religious fanatics and revolutionary fringe groups, terror, as a political tactic, was not invented by twentieth century religious or political extremists. It was a tool used by the government of the French Revolution to discourage resistance. In some areas, a vast number of suspects were indiscriminately killed in order to demonstrate the invincible power of the revolutionary government. It was a tactic that would later be used even more freely by the communist rulers of the Soviet Union and the National Socialists in Germany.

It is not clear how far Saint-Just and his mentor, Robespierre, would have gone in carrying out their plans to recreate a republic of equals. The terror they organized killed so many rival politicians that they were eventually deposed, arrested, and killed (1794). When the more conservative government of the Directory tried to reestablish some semblance of order, the radical theorist Gracchus Babeuf was inspired to organize the "Conspiracy of the Equals." Babeuf and his collaborators—including Filippo (or Philippe) Buonarotti, who would carry the revolutionary torch to a later generation—went beyond earlier plans for equality of property and decided that only a system of communal (that is, state-owned) property could avoid the risk that successful people would eventually own more than the less successful. For the traditional right to property they substituted a right to exist.

Earlier utopians had often reserved a special place for men of learning, but since the cultivation of arts and sciences was also a source of inequality, the Babouvists opposed all higher education that created

Maximilien de Robespierre ruled France as a dictator during the most radical phase of the French Revolution. After sending many of his colleagues and rivals to the guillotine, he himself was guillotined in 1794.

social distinctions. (Some of their anti-intellectualism was obviously borrowed from Rousseau, who had little formal schooling.) Like Saint-Just, Babeuf wanted to weaken the institutions of village and provincial life, imposing on them one great centralized state. Babeuf was unwise enough to publish many of his theories in his newspaper, *Tribun du Peuple* (*The People's Tribune*), and, when the group's "Manifesto of the Equals" was discovered, it proved to be his death sentence. He and a collaborator were executed (May 28, 1796), but others, such as the Italian Filippo Buonarrotti, were simply deported.

AFTER THE DELUGE

On his deathbed King Louis XV of France is supposed to have said, "After me, the deluge," a reference to the catastrophic flood of the book of Genesis. In many ways, the French Revolution was a catastrophe that eliminated the monarchy, traditional aristocracy, the Catholic Church, and all the moral certainties that French society had taken for granted. Other European countries were also suffering secondary shocks from the revolution: There was popular unrest in England, while in Italy secret societies were formed (some under Buonarrotti's inspiration) to end Austrian rule over northern Italy and to overthrow both church and monarchy.

Filippo Buonarroti

A descendant of the painter and sculptor Michelangelo, Filippo Buonarroti was born to a prominent family in Pisa, Italy, in 1761. As a young journalist and political activist eager for revolution, he traveled first to Corsica, where he met the Bonapartes, and then to France. A member of the circle of Gracchus Babeuf, Buonarrotti was exiled after the leaders were arrested. Buonarrotti, though not well-known today, was a key figure in promulgating Masonic and radical ideology and in spreading the idea of communist revolution throughout Europe.

Ordinary people, in a time of crisis, naturally turned to great leaders like Napoleon Bonaparte or to representatives of the old royal family. Deeper thinkers looked for explanations of what had happened and tried to work out new theories of society that would restore order, balance, and security. These thinkers were quite an eccentric bunch: the French Count Saint-Simon, whose family traced its origins back to Charlemagne; Charles Fourier, the son of a French artisan; Robert Owen, a successful English industrialist from a humble background; and Auguste Comte, the student of science and technology who created "Positivism." Of these, it was Comte's positivism that was, for a time, the most serious rival of Marxism. Comte's system, which combined science, economics, and politics, embraced all aspects of human life, and its founder claimed—as Marx would later claim—to have developed a truly scientific approach to social problems.

Although their political systems were quite different, all these men thought they had created a *science* of society based on rules that could be discovered, communicated, and applied. Although some accepted the institution of marriage and family, and others called for a sexual revolution, they all emphasized human brotherhood and tended to look down on individuals and their families as petty. Each of them also believed that the world had been in darkness until he had created his system and that within a few decades the new system would transform the world. All of them, also, firmly believed that a just society, established on scientific principles, would eliminate class conflicts.

Unlike Plato and More, these would-be reformers were not mere theoreticians. Saint-Simon's followers tried to live in their own private community, Fourier called for the creation of phalansteries—small-scale societies in which rigid and uniform equality were practiced (as at Brook Farm in New England)—and Robert Owen used (and lost) a considerable part of his vast personal fortune in setting up the New Harmony colony (1826–1828) in Indiana. All of these experiments came to nothing. The members of the communes were often eccentric, frequently quarreled among themselves, and jockeyed for power. The founders and theorists blamed the bad character of the members, but it is just possible that they had completely misjudged human nature.

French Utopians did make significant contributions to the theory of socialism. Some were opposed to property rights and the family, while the followers of Saint-Simon insisted that each should contribute

Brook Farm

In 1841 George Ripley, a Boston minister, founded a communal colony along the lines of Charles Fourier's utopian socialist philosophy. Many young New England writers and thinkers, dissatisfied with Ralph Waldo Emerson's rejection of Christianity, saw Brook Farm as a way of reconciling socialism with religion. In 1845, the loosely organized colony adopted stricter Fourierite rules. Nathaniel Hawthorne was one of the founders of the colony, which received such distinguished visitors as Ralph Waldo Emerson, Margaret Fuller, and the future newspaper editor and abolitionist, Horace Greeley. The experiment, which asked literary intellectuals to collaborate voluntarily on farm work, suffered the fate of most utopian colonies: unprofitable and divided by personal tensions, it fell apart when the phalanstery, or main house, burned down, before it was completed, in 1846. Brook Farm was neither the first nor the last in a long series of American utopian experiments.

Karl Marx

Karl Marx is the dominant figure of the socialist movement. Born in Trier, Germany, in 1818, he studied classics and law. He eventually adopted the philosophy of materialism, writing his doctoral dissertation on Epicurus, the father of materialism. In 1842 he became the editor of a newspaper (*Rheinisches Zeitung*), which was shut down by the government in the next year. After moving to Paris, he became friends with Friedrich Engels, and the pair became involved in the workers movement and issued *The Communist Manifesto* in 1847, the year before the revolutions of 1848. Forced out of France and then from Belgium, Marx and Engels landed in England, where Marx wrote his major works and helped found the International, an association of workingmen. An irascible intellectual, Marx was very critical of all the writers who influenced him—Adam Smith, Proudhon—and even of his own disciples. Near the end of his life he became so exasperated by their development of his ideas that he told his son-in-law Paul Lafargue, "All I know is I am no Marxist." A complex thinker, Marx is the father of revolutionary communism (Leninism), democratic socialism, and the critical theory of the Frankfurt School.

to society according to his capacity. This idea was later developed by the socialist leader Louis Blanc, who realized that absolute equality could never be attained. For Blanc, social justice meant that each should contribute to society according to his ability and receive according to his needs, an idea that would be appropriated and repeated by Karl Marx, the father of revolutionary communism.

A more serious contribution to socialist theory was provided by the anarchist Pierre-Joseph Proudhon. In his book *What is Property? Or an Inquiry into the Principles of Right and Government* (1840), Proudhon declared, "Property is theft." This idea is perhaps not quite so strange as it first seems. Proudhon accepted the view, common in the eighteenth and nineteenth centuries, that equality was the basis of any just society, but since the institution of private property resulted in great disparities of wealth and power, property was itself the source of inequality. However, unlike the Marxists, Proudhon did not call for the elimination of private property. Instead, he offered an alternative: Property rights should not be absolute, as they had been, but conditional. Property owners who did not put their land to productive use should forfeit their rights.

Karl Marx at first praised Proudhon's argument as a breakthrough, though the two men would later become enemies. Marx preferred public ownership of all the means of production, including agricultural property. Proudhon differed from his rivals in other important ways. Unlike Marx, a German expatriate who called for the end of nation-states, Proudhon was a patriotic Frenchman, and, also, unlike Marx and Engels, who saw the traditional family as oppressive, Proudhon broke with the utopians and exempted the family from the strict regulation he imposed on other institutions.

During the communist heyday of the Soviet Union, most socialists would have said that Marx had the better of the argument, but in large capitalist nations like the United States, ownership of property is increasingly dependent upon political decisions, and, under the laws of eminent domain, private property may now be seized and sold or given to another private owner, so long as the new owner will make a more significant contribution to the local economy. Proudhon's view of property has apparently triumphed, and his attachment to nation and family no longer seems so old-fashioned or sentimental, since both have survived revolutionary capitalism and democratic socialism.

MARX AND ENGELS

By far the most important contributions to nineteenth century socialist theory were made by two Germans who spent much of their lives in England: Karl Marx and his friend and disciple Friedrich Engels. Both men were involved in the revolutionary struggles that engulfed Europe in the 1830s and 1840s. One year before the great revolutionary year of 1848, they were leaders of a small group of German radicals in whose name they published the *Communist Manifesto*, which offers a somewhat simple analysis of history as the story of class conflict and concludes with a stirring appeal to revolutionary violence.

"The history of all hitherto existing society," declared Marx and Engels, "is the history of class struggles." Ancient Rome, the Middle Ages, and capitalist Europe all pitted rich against poor, exploiters against workers. With the discovery of the New World and the expansion of markets, the bourgeoisie—that is, the middle-class owners of business interests—expanded their power and wealth at the expense of the old authorities of monarchy, aristocracy, and the Church, but the day was coming when even the nation-states created by the bourgeoisie would themselves be destroyed by the proletariat, that is, the impoverished working class uprooted from all local traditions and networks and exploited by the bourgeois owners of mines and factories.

> The weapons with which the bourgeoisie felled feudalism
> to the ground are now turned against the bourgeoisie
> itself. But not only has the bourgeoisie forged the weapons
> that bring death to itself; it has also called into existence
> the men who are to wield those weapons—the modern
> working class—the proletarians.

Nation-states are doomed because "working men have no country," and the bourgeois family—which exploits working-class women—is also slated for extinction.

The *Manifesto* goes on to explain that, while many parties and movements were calling for reform of national economic systems, only communists like Marx, Engels, and their followers realized that private property and the nation-state were both doomed. While other socialist movements pandered either to the bourgeoisie or to the old

Karl Marx and Friedrich Engels were the founders of what was first known as scientific socialism. Together they worked out a comprehensive economic and political theory of class conflict, and helped to establish socialist movements in Europe.

aristocracy or to national governments, communists realized that the upper classes—along with marriage, the family, and the state—were slated for extinction. Marx and Engels believed that democratic reform movements were nothing more than what we would today call Band-Aids. The only solution was violent revolution, which had to be pursued openly:

> The Communists disdain to conceal their views and aims. They openly declare that their ends can be attained only by the forcible overthrow of all existing social conditions. Let the ruling classes tremble at a communist revolution. The proletarians have nothing to lose but their chains. They have a world to win. Proletarians of all countries, unite!

This was powerful rhetoric in 1847, and it still makes a strong appeal to the imagination. The *Manifesto* became the blueprint for revolutionary communism, but its major points—class conflict, capitalist exploitation of the working classes, the need for global economic justice—were to be incorporated into the programs of most democratic socialist parties and movements. In his early years Marx was unable to prove either his sweeping view of history (derived in part from the philosopher Georg Wilhelm Fredrich Hegel) or his economic theories. He and Engels spent the rest of their lives, when they were not organizing their movement—the First International, an association of workingmen, was founded in London in 1864—working out the details of their theories.

The three great principles of Marxism are: 1) a materialist and economic interpretation of history; 2) Marx's theory that class struggle is the dominant note of human history; and 3) Marx's version of the labor theory of value. The first two principles go together. Avoiding earlier theories of history that emphasized the role of divine providence, the impact of great men and their rivalries, or the influence of geography, Marx looked for a scientific explanation of historical change and found it in the human need to acquire and thus to produce and exchange the material necessities required for existence. Diverse forms of production (for example, different types of farming) lead to different types of societies. As he wrote, "The means of production in material life determines the general character of the social, political, and spiritual processes of life." Since the rich were able to command the labor and resources of the poor, the competition for the necessities of life also lead to a never-ending class struggle.

Capitalism, which was the greatest revolutionary force in the history of the world, would inevitably destroy itself because as capitalism developed it became ever more efficient. By capitalism, he meant a system of manufacturing in which the means of production were owned and controlled by a small class of investors. Marx believed that capitalism would concentrate more and more manufacturing in the hands of fewer and fewer owners, and by increasing efficiency it would employ fewer and fewer workers, whose competition for jobs then would reduce their wages to the lowest level. This would lead ultimately to revolution. On the basis of such theories, Marx supported the Union cause in the American Civil War, because the victory of the bourgeois North would hasten the ultimate self-destruction of capitalism.

Marx's greatest work was *Capital*, a response to the classical (free-market) economic theories of Adam Smith and David Ricardo (a theoretical and practicing capitalist), but his theories are also worked out in his *Critique of Political Economy*. A complex and difficult work, *Capital* sets out to prove and refine the classical economic theory that value is determined by the amount of labor that goes into producing goods. In very simple terms, the value of a wooden spoon is determined by the cost of cutting (and perhaps growing) the tree and the cost of the labor that went into making the spoon. The cost of labor, according to Marx, should not be measured by the actual hours it might take any one person, but the rate at which a skilled worker worked, using the best available technology. While it might take an unskilled worker, using hand tools, several hours to fashion a spoon, a skilled craftsman might take ten minutes, working by hand, and a mere second if operating a machine. The labor component of the value would then be determined by the machine operator's one second of work. Profit to the capitalist came when he paid, for example, one cent for the wood, another cent for use of his machinery, and ten cents for the labor, but sold the spoon for twenty cents. Capitalists called it profit. Marx called it exploitation.

The Labor Theory of Value is an improvement upon older theories that based value either on precious metals or on agricultural commodities. Capitalist economists, although they created and developed the theory, were cautious about using it to explain how prices were set. Smith concluded that such an approach was workable only in a primitive economy because in a developed economic system the price included some amount of profit for the owner. Capitalist economist Ricardo, on the other hand, stipulated that value did not derive from a worker's wages but from the amount of work itself. For Marx and Engels the theory was a moral imperative to be applied as soon as a socialist state was formed. The owners' excessive profits were proof that they were exploiting the workers.

The most obvious difficulty with the Marxist version of the theory is that it is virtually impossible to apply it. It is not just the fact that some people work more efficiently than others—Marx knew as much—but that the productive capacity of a scientist or entrepreneur cannot be reduced to a simplistic formula. An inventor might think about a problem for two years with no results but find a solution worth tens of millions of dollars to someone, after five minutes in the shower. The founder of the Austrian School of economics, Carl Menger, later proposed a subjective theory of value, which says that value is determined solely by an individual's desire for a particular good. The more you want something—and the harder it is to obtain—the more you are willing to pay for it. This is most obvious in the high prices charged for the junk of a previous generation or the high cost of tickets for pop music concerts. It takes two, however, to make a market. As a farmer you may value your potatoes at one hundred dollars a pound but unless others share your perception, you will never find a buyer. It is only when the subjective values of seller and buyer converge that products can be sold.

The Subjective Theory of Value is probably the most appropriate way of evaluating market prices, but it presents its own set of problems. If economic value is simply a matter of what I happen to be willing to pay (or the average of what one million "I's" will pay), why is the same not true of aesthetic and moral judgments? Many people would agree that it makes no difference that you like Mozart and I like Madonna, but most would balk at the idea that it also makes no difference whether you like gardening and I prefer mass murder. This is a simplistic example, which liberals would reject because it involves violence or coercion, but what about suicide or voluntary cannibalism or sexual relations with consenting minors? One person's question of taste might be another person's moral taboo. Value subjectivity, as useful a tool as it can be, illustrates one of the main tendencies of liberalism, which is toward value-neutrality and amorality.

Marx was wrong in thinking that value could be determined by abstract calculations, but classical liberals may be even more dangerously wrong in thinking that all value is based on an individual's subjective preference. In fact, most individual preferences are determined not by individuals but by families, friends, communities, social fashions, and local and national traditions. Few of us can remember how and when we decided we liked chocolate ice cream more than strawberry or took a dislike to blues or Baroque music, but our individual tastes most often reflect the influence of other people or of an entire society. In this sense, Marxists were not entirely wrong to search for a social basis of value.

Engels thought that the people of a socialist society would quite easily determine the value of labor and the price of goods. Experience has shown this expectation to be extremely naïve. As a businessman, Engels might be expected to have been more practical than Marx, and in later life he did adapt his views to changing circumstances. Although less influential than his friend, Engels made several important contributions to socialist thought: a grim account of England's poor, *The Condition of the Working Class in England* (1844), as well as an influential theoretical work, *The Origin of the Family, Private Property, and the State* (1884), in which he argued (with a limited knowledge of history and anthropology) that all three—family, property, and the state—were invented by greedy patriarchal males who seized power over women, invented property rights, and, by establishing a monopoly of violence, used the institutions of government to protect their power and property. Although Engels' theory has been taken seriously only by Marxist anthropologists, it is a brilliant piece of propaganda that has profoundly influenced many social and political movements, feminism in particular.

The First International broke up as a result of feuding and power struggles among the followers of Proudhon, Marx, and the Russian anarchist Mikhail Bakunin. After Marx's death (1883), Engels admitted that they had been hasty in predicting a communist revolution. Quite the opposite happened. Though socialists were spreading and gaining respectability, capitalism showed no signs of collapsing. As bad as their timing was, it would not be many decades before socialist principles would rise to the top of many political agendas.

PRAGMATIC SOCIALISM IN BRITAIN AND GERMANY

Marxist historians have sometimes overemphasized the influence of Marx on the development of socialism in nineteenth-century Britain.

Outside of Germany, few people could read German, and Marx's works were not translated into English until after his death. Marx did not create the socialist movement, though he did contribute its most comprehensive theoretical justification. Quite independently of theoretical socialism, English workers were organizing trade unions and demanding higher wages and better working conditions. Trade unions, however, were illegal until 1871, which tended to make workers somewhat hostile toward the government. Lacking the right to vote as well as the right to strike, the workers' only recourses were illegal (sometimes violent) strikes, public demonstrations, and protests to Parliament. The most popular and influential protest movement was known as Chartism (founded in 1838) because the members gathered hundreds of thousands of signatures for a six-point "People's charter," calling for universal male suffrage with no property qualifications. Rather than pursue violent revolution or even public demonstrations, the Chartists realized that workingmen, if they wished to improve their position, needed to work through the political process and to do that they needed the right to vote. The Chartists failed in the short run, but all of their demands were eventually granted by democratically elected parliaments.

Another influential movement in the decade before World War I was Guild Socialism. Inspired by visions of medieval guilds and by the writings of John Ruskin, Guild Socialists did not seek political power or economic equality but the empowerment of workers and the restoration of older traditions of community and cooperation. Instead of using the dislocated proletariat as a revolutionary army, they wished to restore some of the stability of community and vocation that capitalism had eliminated. Although as socialists they wanted "public ownership" of industries, they were opposed to the creation of managerial bureaucracies. Guild Socialists were different in another important respect: they were as interested in high standards of craftsmanship as in high wages. Their slogan, "self-government in industry," popularized in the writings of G. D. H. Cole, appealed to some liberals, who would have rejected Marx's call for revolution. However, it is hard to see how their objectives could have been achieved without the development of the government apparatus that has typified socialist states.

British socialists in the late nineteenth century began to turn away from violent revolution and toward democratic reform. They tended to reject utopian theories and to concentrate on pragmatic, technical solutions, which required an educated class of managers and leaders. One important sign of the change was the creation (in 1884) of the Fabian Society. The members included leading British radicals, intellectuals, and writers. The guiding spirits were Beatrice and Sydney Webb and the playwright George Bernard Shaw. Taking their name from Fabius, a famous Roman general who saved Rome not by confronting, but by stalling Hannibal and the Carthaginians, the Fabians relied on public persuasion and regular political tactics as the best means of introducing socialism. Although Shaw remained critical of Marx, the Webbs became communists late in life. The Fabian Society, however, as early as 1887 proclaimed itself socialist and called for "the reorganization of society by the emancipation of land and industrial capital from individual and class ownership."

The Fabians had little interest in a mass movement, nor did they wish to empower workers. On the contrary, they saw themselves as something like Plato's Guardians, who made it possible for a communistic society to function. When Shaw was asked when the workers would manage the factories, he replied contemptuously: "When they write their own plays." The Fabians may have believed in economic and social equality, but they refused to abandon their belief in the superiority of intellectuals.

About the same time in Germany, Eduard Bernstein, a German Marxist who had made friends with Engels in London, developed the gradualist or revisionist wing of European socialism. Rejecting Marx's analysis of class conflict and call for revolution, Bernstein argued that the workers would gradually win the concessions they needed without directly overthrowing the capitalist system. Unlike most socialists, Bernstein understood that socialism, rather than being in conflict with basic liberal principles, could be seen as an extension of them. Liberals had worked to end restrictions imposed by religion and aristocracy. What remained was to end the oppression based on wealth, and this could only be done by gradual and democratic means.

GRADUAL REFORM OR VIOLENT REVOLUTION

In the two decades following Marx's death, the socialist movement went in two opposite directions. The communists, especially Russians like N. Lenin and Leon Trotsky, continued to plot revolution. Fabians and revisionists laid plans to transform capitalist systems from within. In one of the many factional disputes among Russian socialists (or social democrats), Lenin and his friends claimed a majority and were afterward known as the Bolsheviks (that is, the majority party), although their opponents the Mensheviks (the minority) often had as many, if not more, members. By the end of 1917 Lenin and his Bolshevik party had taken over the Russian Revolution and were well on the way to establishing the first communist state, the Union of the Soviet Socialist Republics (U.S.S.R.).

Although Lenin was regarded as an orthodox Marxist, he contributed important concepts to socialist and communist theory. Lenin emphasized the importance of a global and continuous revolutionary struggle to rid the world of capitalism. To accomplish this task, Lenin reorganized the Communist Party (as opposed to the nation-state) as the structural embodiment of the revolution, and in 1920 through the Comintern (Communist International) he imposed a uniform set of twenty-one requirements on any affiliated party. After Lenin's death, Josef Stalin, without abandoning global revolution as the ultimate goal, wanted to build up Russia as a fortress of the Communist Party under the slogan "socialism within one country." His chief rival, Trotsky, was more of an internationalist, but he was driven into exile and eventually murdered on Stalin's orders.

Although no one could deny Lenin's success, the Fabians and gradualists did not relax their efforts to introduce socialism by democratic means. A little in awe of the Russian communists' triumph, they confined their criticisms of the U.S.S.R. to details and methods and shut their eyes to the mass starvation and brutal massacres perpetrated already in Lenin's time and at an increased pace with the accession of Stalin in 1924. In the 1928 edition of *The Intelligent Woman's Guide to Socialism*, Shaw declared that the Soviet Union was a success story—an extraordinary delusion in so intelligent a man. Nonetheless, the years after the end of World War I were witness to the increasing power of socialist movements and parties in England, France, Germany, and much of the rest of Europe. The history and organization of communist states is not the focus of this book, but it is worth pointing out that after the collapse of the U.S.S.R. and the general discrediting of communism, socialist principles have remained an essential part of *all* major political parties in the West.

THE TWENTIETH CENTURY SOCIALIST AGENDA

By the end of World War I in 1918, socialist ideas had been expressed in many different forms and embraced by a variety of movements and parties. Agrarian parties, for example, demanded more land for poor farmers, while trade unions continued to strive for higher wages, pensions, and better working conditions. European politics between the two world wars would be a struggle between two antagonistic types of socialism, both owing a great deal to Marx: internationalist communism and the national socialisms that developed in Germany (Nazi Party), Spain (Falange Español), and Italy (Fascist Party). Although national socialist parties did include right-wing elements—especially a belief in the nation and its traditions—their domestic policies were primarily socialist. Before turning to fascism, Mussolini had been a leader in the Italian Socialist Party, and Adolf Hitler more than once acknowledged his debt to Marx. The socialist elements in national socialism and fascism were rooted in the anti-liberal premise that the state was not merely an umpire or honest broker that punished crime and enforced contracts, but an all-powerful parent of the nation that had a major responsibility to provide for the welfare of the people. Needless to say, the Nazis did not live up to their promises.

Socialism was evolving in this period, and it has continued to evolve. Trotsky and his followers remained faithful to the ideal of "permanent revolution" and looked for opportunities in the developing world. In a crude way, Trotsky also took an ideological interest in literature and the arts, which he saw as a battlefield for what would become known as the "culture wars." A deeper cultural revolutionary was the Italian Marxist Antonio Gramsci, one of the most influential socialist thinkers of the twentieth century. Sent to prison (where he died in 1937) by Mussolini, Gramsci set out to analyze the means by which a ruling class achieves *hegemony* (dominant ruling authority). This sort of analysis goes back to an Italian tradition of thought that began with Nicolò Machiavelli and was elaborated by such political theorists as Gaetano Mosca and Vilfredo Pareto. Gramsci argued that capitalists had consolidated their hegemony by taking over and maintaining cultural institutions, such as schools, universities, and churches, and for socialists to succeed they had to infiltrate and subvert these institutions, turning them to socialist purposes.

This cultural approach, which would later be called "the long march through the institutions," was adopted by a number of important radical intellectuals, most famously by the leaders of the so-called Frankfurt

School, Max Horkheimer and Theodor Adorno, and their disciples Jürgen Habermas and Herbert Marcuse. Through his books (such as *One Dimensional Man*) and his university teaching, Marcuse had a great impact on radical students in the United States. Members of the Frankfurt School in the 1930s and its later incarnation at the New School for Social Research in New York used their "critical theory" (combining Marx's early writings with psychoanalysis) not only to examine social institutions and artistic traditions, but also to change them. Their criticism of the family, for example, and of what they called the "authoritarian personality" was part of a campaign to undermine the bourgeois family and the engrained habit of loyalty and respect, which (they believed) characterized the German people.

By the 1920s and 1930s socialism had assumed many forms, some of them quite antagonistic to each other. Nevertheless most socialist programs put forward by political parties contain certain constant themes.

Economic. Socialists have advocated national ownership, control, and regulation of the most important means of production (mines and factories), transportation (highways, railroads, airlines), and communication (telegraph, telephone, radio, and television); economic control of wages and prices, as in the minimum-wage standards that exist in most developed countries today; and redistribution of income from the more to the less wealthy, usually by means of stiff taxes on inheritance and graduated income taxes.

Social. To achieve equality, socialists and their imitators have introduced social insurance for the sick (national health care), the elderly (pensions and social security), state assistance and protection for children, which required a corresponding lessening of the responsibility and authority of parents. This goal had already been approached by establishing national educational systems, but additional programs were gradually added: the prohibition of child labor, child protection and delinquency laws, and guaranteed maternity leave for working mothers.

Global. Finally, socialist governments worked to dismantle colonial empires, called for subsidies to be sent from rich countries to poor countries, and, except in the case of national socialist parties in the 1930s and 1940s, believed in international cooperation (through the League of Nations, the United Nations, the World Bank, and the World Trade Organization) with the ultimate goal, already anticipated by the *Communist Manifesto*, of world government.

The history of the twentieth century can be viewed as a struggle among conflicting theories of socialism: the violent revolution preached by communist leaders such as Lenin, Stalin, and Mao; the gradualist model advocated by democratic socialists like Bernstein and the Fabians; the combination of nationalism and socialism that produced the Nazi Party, and influenced the leaders of many developing nations, such as Juan Perón in Chile, and Gamal Abdel Nasser in Egypt; and finally the welfare-state capitalism practiced by free-market countries like the United States. In time, especially after the collapse of the Soviet empire, these socialist systems began to converge with each other and merge with other more conservative movements. Thus, it should not be too surprising that the French socialist political leader François Mitterand began his career as a nationalist supporter of France's conservative Vichy government, which was allied with Nazi Germany. Even as a socialist, Mitterand seemed more of a nationalist than a classic socialist, though he certainly advocated and enacted socialist policies.

Socialism, then, although it might conceivably exist in a theoretically pure form, has rarely exhibited itself in the real world except as a tendency. To gain a real appreciation of socialism, we have to examine the concrete forms of this tendency, as expressed in such diverse countries as Britain and Sweden, Yugoslavia and Mexico. It is only by sampling some of the particular flavors of the various socialist experiments that we can begin to develop a comprehensive view.

3
Socialist Economies

ALTHOUGH THE HOUSE OF SOCIALISM has many rooms, the main room—the living room shown off to visitors—is a socialized economic system. Most socialists have accepted Marx's theory that human history is a seemingly endless conflict between the exploiting upper class and the exploited lower classes. Translated into concrete political terms, class conflict is a problem that can only be remedied by vast state-directed alterations of economic structures. The ultimate object is economic justice, and that object, in the absence of violent revolution, will be attained by enacting a wide array of socialist policies, from the graduated income tax to collectivized farming. Whether socialist means are an effective way of reaching socialist objectives remains to be seen.

The Marxists who founded the Second International in Paris (1889) on the centenary of the French Revolution said their object was the emancipation of workers and the abolition of wage-slavery. This emancipation would come to include specific demands for the eight-hour day, equalized incomes for workers and managers, retirement pensions, subsidized (or free) health care, and equal employment opportunities (and salaries) regardless of sex. To achieve these goals, some socialist governments have attempted to implement the Marxist theory that the means of production (factories and agricultural land) must be owned by the state. Others have sought to achieve equality by redistributing wealth and incomes and by establishing state systems to provide health care and ensure welfare for all citizens. While the means may change, the main objective remains the same: progress toward economic equality.

EQUALIZING OUTCOMES: GERMANY

The goal of economic equality has proved to be more difficult to achieve than socialists first believed. While communist states confiscated property and wealth, and democratic socialist states have devised complex systems of wealth transfer, neither approach has actually eliminated class distinction. Some of the more obvious egalitarian measures that have come to be taken for granted are: steep taxes on inheritance to discourage the creation of large family fortunes, the graduated income tax, which sets tax rates (theoretically) in proportion to income, wage and price controls to prevent or control inflation, minimum-wage standards and an eight-hour workday, free education and health care, and state pensions for the elderly and disabled. Not all of these policies have been promoted under the socialist banner, but all are derived from socialist theories that regard vast disparities of wealth as inherently unjust.

From the beginning, equalization policies met with stiff resistance. The German failure in the years between the two world wars is instructive. Europe's oldest and most important socialist party, the German Social Democratic Party (SDP), was founded in 1863 by the prominent German intellectual Ferdinand Lasalle as the "German General Workers Association" (ADAV), which merged with the more strictly Marxist Social Democratic Workers Party in 1875, before splitting again in the twentieth century. Prohibited in 1878, the party was legalized again in 1890 and a year later adopted the name it bears today, when it is again the largest party in Germany. In the early years the SDP's theoreticians followed a radical line, calling for nationalization of major industries; however, its tactics were more in tune with the democratic and "gradualist" position of Eduard Bernstein. Bernstein, nonetheless, condemned the SDP for its Marxist theories and radical rhetoric.

In the election of 1912 the party won nearly 35 percent of the vote, the first really impressive electoral showing for an openly socialist party. As the oldest and most prestigious socialist party in Europe, the SDP became a model for other parties. Part of the party's prestige came from the influence of such leaders as August Bebel, the party's leader and an advocate of women's rights, and Karl Kautsky, who was seen, after Engels' death, as the greatest political theorist on the left.

After Germany's defeat in World War I, the Kaiser was deposed, and the government (1919–1933) came under the intermittent control of Social Democrats in coalition with liberal parties. The leaders of the SDP wasted much of their energy in internal struggles and in conflicts with the German Communist Party, which declared its loyalty to the Russian-controlled Third International, or Comintern. In return for Russian support, however, the Comintern laid down twenty-one strict conditions for membership, which took away much of the independence of the member parties. This division of socialists between Comintern (later Cominform) parties and independent socialist parties would continue down to the end of the Cold War.

Although the Social Democrats were challenged by general strikes and revolutionary violence, they managed to form governments (1918–1920 and 1928–1932) that wrestled with major problems of unemployment, inflation, and the reparations Germany was required to pay her victorious allies. An even more serious challenge emerged in the form of the National Socialist German Workers Party, which combined national resentments against German surrender at the end of World War I with a somewhat unspecific appeal to the patriotic members of the working classes. Under the circumstances, it is not entirely strange that the socialists, who enacted few positive programs, found themselves displaced by more conservative and more radical parties, whose conflicts paved the way for the rise of Adolf Hitler and the Nazi Party. Before being outlawed by the Nazis in 1933, the Social Democrats did cast a vote—the only party to do so—against the act that gave power to Hitler. It was the party's proudest moment.

The SDP, during the years of imperial Germany and the Weimar Republic, presents something of a paradox. Failing to enact socialist policies through the government, the party was itself a model socialist society whose members were provided with reading rooms, places to eat, drink, and exercise, as well as chess clubs, women's groups, and choral ensembles. The party also offered support for the sick and elderly. It was an excellent model for voluntary, communitarian socialism, though not, perhaps, a model that could be adapted to the needs of a large modern state. The failure of the SDP may be due in part to the fact that it had gotten stuck in its impractical rhetoric and gained power before it had outlined a pragmatic party program. After World War II, the party would gradually reestablish itself, first as the major opposition party and then eventually as Germany's ruling party for many years. By then it had dropped its extreme rhetoric and concentrated on practical programs.

SOCIALIZING PROPERTY AND INDUSTRY: MEXICO

Most socialist parties came into existence advocating collective ownership of the means of production. To accomplish this goal, socialists advocated large-scale confiscation of industries and agricultural property, with or without compensation to the former owners. Revolutionary states, such as the U.S.S.R., China, and (to a lesser degree) Yugoslavia and Mexico did enact policies of uncompensated nationalization, not only of industries but also of agricultural property. Nationalization has not been, in general, a successful experiment, and in the extreme cases the price tag for collectivized farming in the U.S.S.R., China, and Cambodia was mass starvation and the loss of tens of millions of lives.

In Mexico, the revolution began as a revolt against the dictator Porfirio Díaz and culminated in a rejection of the predominantly Spanish ruling class and a redefinition of Mexico as a Native American country (as opposed to a postcolonial Spanish state shaped by four centuries of Spanish rule). The revolution, in other words, was about everything but Marxism, though some revolutionary leaders, especially Emiliano Zapata, called for a massive redistribution of land back to the native peasants and their village communes.

The revolutionaries who drafted the Constitution of 1917 declared that the land was originally owned by the nation and that only "Mexicans by birth or naturalization and Mexican companies have the right to acquire ownership of lands, waters, and their appurtenances." This controversial article (number 27) legitimized two radical measures. First, it made possible the appropriation of land that allegedly had been stolen from peasants and native tribes; second, it paved the way for the nationalization of land or businesses owned by foreign individuals, companies, or countries. As one recent Mexican historian has written, "Only the Bolshevik Revolution would go further."

Even before the adoption of the Constitution of 1917, President Francisco Madero had begun a reorganization of agriculture that included some expropriation of property. Unproductive farm land was the particular target of his successors, but in the 1930s President Lázaro

Emiliano Zapata
1879–1919

A leading actor in the Mexican Revolution, Emiliano Zapata was a controversial figure. While his enemies portrayed him as a bandit chieftain like Pancho Villa, his admirers—and there are many even today in the state of Chiapas—regard him as a high-minded and selfless reformer. Born to a family of independent but by no means wealthy farmers, Zapata by the age of thirty had become head of his village's defense force. In 1910 he joined the revolution against the dictator Diaz and became a noted guerrilla commander. Unlike many warlords of the revolutionary movement, Zapata proclaimed a sweeping social plan ("The Plan of Ayala") and called for "land, liberty, and justice." Zapata turned against every revolutionary leader who came to power as Mexican president, claiming each was betraying the cause of the revolution. He declared repeatedly that he did not want the presidency for himself, only the power to improve the lot of the indigenous peasants of his province. Treacherously lured into a meeting with a representative of President Venustiano Carranza, Zapata was shot to death, but he has been revered to this day as a superhuman hero who fought tirelessly for justice. The "Zapatista" movement in Chiapas, which has more than once risen in armed rebellion, takes its name from the slain leader.

Pancho Villa and Emiliano Zapata are caught in an historic moment of the Mexican Revolution. Ex-bandit Villa (*left*) sits in the president's chair while Zapata, the leader of the revolt, looks on uncomfortably. Both were eventually gunned down by rivals.

Cárdenas, who had decided to cash in some of the nationalization chips the government was holding, embarked on a vast agrarian reform program that confiscated land—even productive estates—and converted them to *ejidos*, collective farms that are communally owned and worked by the peasants.

Mexican railroads had already been nationalized in 1907, and in 1935 President Cárdenas declared that private (often foreign) ownership of the oil industry was not consistent with the constitution, though he subsequently promised the U.S. ambassador that he would not nationalize either mining or oil. When labor unrest shut down oil production, the president appointed a special commission that ended by decreeing that higher wages and damages be paid the workers. Standard Oil, confident that Mexico would not stand up to the United States, refused, and, after protracted, often bitter, negotiations, Cárdenas nationalized Mexico's petroleum reserves and confiscated foreign-owned equipment (March 1938). Despite a British and U.S. boycott, Cárdenas' maneuver succeeded because the United States preferred to buy Mexican oil rather than see it go to Nazi Germany.

Mexico went through several more rounds of nationalization, and by 1982 the government owned more than 1,100 businesses. However, most state-owned industries proved to be unproductive, and beginning in the 1980s the government undertook a vigorous campaign of privatization. The program has caused the loss of hundreds of thousands of jobs and, predictably, put valuable resources into the hands of influential members of Mexico's elite classes. A similar story can be told in many postcommunist (Russia) and democratic (Italy) countries—though not, for example, in Britain. Nationalization creates inefficiency and corruption, while privatization, rather than being a remedy, is often an opportunity for further corruption.

Some democratic-socialist parties in Europe learned that such programs were unlikely to attract votes from independent tradesmen, shopkeepers, or even from comparatively prosperous skilled laborers. On the other hand, when countries such as Britain and Italy nationalized large industries and compensated the owners, it was not many decades before the inefficiency of government-run enterprises became so glaringly apparent that they had to begin the process of privatization. The same lesson was learned even more painfully by Eastern European states after the collapse of communism.

NATIONALIZATION: THE BRITISH LABOUR PARTY

During this same interwar period, the leaders of the British Labour Party, although they fared little better than the German SDP in passing socialist legislation, were gaining vital practical experience in the business of governing. Founded as the Independent Labour Party in 1893, the party represented a coalition of trade unions and more theoretical socialists, such as the Fabians. A few trade unionists, such as the former miner James Keir Hardie, had already been elected to Parliament, but the new party hoped to coordinate the unions' political efforts. J. Ramsay MacDonald, a working class Fabian from Scotland, joined the party in 1894 and, after winning a seat in Parliament, rose to the top of the party.

From the first, union issues were paramount, though union members were not especially eager to abandon the Liberal Party, which had given them the vote and the right to organize, or to take their chances with the inexperienced Labour Party. But when a British court held the railway union liable for losses suffered by the Taff Vale Railway during a strike, voters flocked to the new party in the general election of 1906. Labour members of Parliament (MPs) succeeded in passing the Trade Disputes Act, which ensured the right to strike. That was virtually the only major Labour Party victory before World

War I, as economic troubles and the threat of war occupied British attention. Immediately after World War I, the party demanded a full-scale transformation of British society. As their manifesto declared, the "individualist system of capitalist production, based on private ownership and competitive administration of land and capital, with its reckless profiteering" had to be replaced by "a deliberately planned co-operation in production and distribution for the benefit of all who participate." This was not, the Labour Party assured the people, a program for revolution, but a goal to be achieved by a gradual democratic process.

Many British socialists had been opposed to World War I, and their pacifism cost several Labour Party members (including MacDonald) their seats in Parliament. However, the collapse of the Liberal Party in the 1920s made the Labour Party the only serious rival to the Conservatives, who adopted much of the Liberal Party's free-market economic agenda. MacDonald was prime minister (PM) in 1924–1926 and 1929–1935, but since the Labour Party never had a majority of seats, they had to rely first on the support of Liberals, who opposed socialist legislation, and, after 1930, on the Conservatives who dominated MacDonald's cabinet ministry. MacDonald did succeed in passing the Wheatley Housing Act, which built 50,000 low-cost houses, but, in general, further progress in socialist legislation was postponed by the Great Depression and by World War II.

During the war, however, Winston Churchill's coalition government, which included prominent Labourites, acquired emergency powers to set wages and prices and to oversee the entire British economy. These measures were a solid foundation for the socialist programs adopted by Labour Party governments after the war. Churchill himself had advocated a wide array of measures, which, if adopted, would have amounted to a Conservative Party version of the welfare state. The main issue in the election of 1945, therefore, was not whether or not to enact socialist programs, but which party was more likely to make a good job of them. Other postwar conservative leaders in Europe, including Alcide de Gasperi, head of the Christian Democratic Party in Italy, were similarly inclined to reject free-market capitalism and to accept major parts of the socialist program.

After the Labour Party's landslide victory in the election of 1945 (393 Labour members to 197 Conservatives), the government of Prime Minister Clement Atlee (1945–1951) accomplished a legal socialist

Clement Atlee

Clement Richard Atlee, a university-educated barrister (trial lawyer), was a leader of the British Labour Party and prime minister (1945–1951). Wounded in World War I, Atlee taught at the London School of Economics and became mayor of London. As opposition leader he served throughout World War II as an important member of Winston Churchill's cabinet. Elected by a landslide over Churchill, Atlee proceeded to implement Keynesian economic policies and a variety of socialist measures, including nationalization of industries, national health service, and the breakup of the British colonial empire. Although many of his policies have been reversed, he is still regarded by British academics as the most successful peacetime prime minister of the twentieth century. Defeated in 1951, he returned to the House of Commons until 1955 when he was elevated to the peerage as Earl Atlee and entered the House of Lords. He died in 1967, leaving an estate that was surprisingly modest for any party leader.

revolution. Preserving the centralized economic planning that had been adopted during the war, Atlee's government was able to nationalize the previously private Bank of England, iron and steel production, the coal and gas industries, electricity, the radio and telegraph services, and much of the rail and transport system. Nationalization had been a Labour Party objective since the Fabian Sidney Webb authored the famous Clause Four of the party's constitution:

> To secure for the workers by hand or by brain the full fruits of their industry and the most equitable distribution thereof that may be possible upon the basis of the common ownership of the means of production, distribution, and exchange, and the best obtainable system of popular administration and control of each industry or service.

Labourites justified all these takings on practical grounds. According to the 1945 manifesto *Let Us Face the Future*, nationalizing the Bank of England would reduce unemployment, while taking over coal, gas, and electricity production would help to modernize the economy.

Although Marxist and Fabian socialists had called for confiscation without compensation, the British government paid for the property and businesses it acquired. The stock of publicly traded companies was exchanged for government bonds of the same face value. The prices paid were not small: The cost of acquiring the coal industry was roughly $5 billion U.S. (in 2006 dollars).

Everything was done to secure an orderly transition. To manage the new entities, boards and managers were made up of former directors and managers, as well as union officials. Marxists complained that too much was done to ensure continuity and placate the capitalists. A more serious criticism has been made that nationalization did not produce the results the Labour Party had so confidently predicted. Convinced that private enterprise was a bad thing, the planners in the party apparently took it for granted that large corporations, put under the control of democratic governments, would automatically pursue more socially constructive policies. That did not happen; managers were still managers, only, without any stake in profits or growth, much less enterprising.

In 1907 the English social critic W. H. Mallock had predicted the consequences of what he regarded as the best possible scheme of nationalization, in which capitalists managed socially owned industries. Though they lost the profit incentive, their training and experience would still make them efficient managers, but when the first generation died off, it would be impossible to find men of equal ability who would manage effectively without the usual enticement of profit and advancement. In other words, efficient management must always take the profit motive and human ambition into account.

NATIONALIZATION IN EUROPE AND THE UNITED STATES

Problems lay in the future, but Britain's orderly and legal approach to nationalization helped inspire other socialist parties to embark on similar programs of nationalization. In the late 1940s and 1950s, Austria, with the support of the United States (but over the protest of the U.S.S.R.!), succeeded in nationalizing 22 percent of the nation's industry. In France, between 1945 and 1948, coalition governments nationalized coal, insurance, gas and electricity, the merchant fleet, the Banque de France and several other important banking institutions, Air France, and the Renault car manufacturing company. Some of the nationalization was revenge against industries believed to have cooperated with France's pro-German Vichy government during the war, but France, even under a nonsocialist leader like Charles de Gaulle, was going with the socialist flow. A similar story can be told of Italy.

In Scandinavia, however, socialist governments preferred to work *with*, not *against* business, and the focus was put on cooperative planning boards that included representatives from government, business, and labor, who together worked to eliminate the conflict between capital and labor that led to costly strikes. In occupied Germany both the SDP and the conservative Christian Democratic Union (CDU) supported the nationalization of mines and heavy industries, but the Americans, with a traditional suspicion of socialism, refused to do the same.

The United States has developed its own tradition of democratic socialism but rarely under that name. The Socialist Party of America (SPA) was formed from two preexisting parties in 1901, and while the party succeeded in winning many mayoral elections and sending two

Eugene Debs, the leader of the U.S. Socialist Party, opposed the entrance of the United States into World War I. A successful labor organizer, Debs was unfairly jailed during a railway strike. While he was in jail, he read Marx and became a socialist.

members to Congress, it has rarely played a major role in national elections. The SPA's most popular and effective leader, former railroad worker Eugene V. Debs, was convicted and sent to jail in 1918 for openly opposing World War I. Radical union leader "Big Bill" Heywood was also sent to jail because his union, the Industrial Workers of the World, had printed antiwar pamphlets before the entrance of the United States into the war, but never circulated them. Debs garnered 6 percent of the vote in the presidential election of 1912, but after the war, the fear of bolshevism marginalized the socialists. In 1928 the Socialist Party chose Norman Thomas, a Presbyterian minister, as its leader, and he caused his party to take a firm stand in favor of democracy and against the U.S.S.R. Though Thomas never came close to winning an election, he lived long enough to see most of his socialist policies enacted by Democrats and Republicans.

The United States government has never embarked on an openly socialist program of nationalization, though the government has confiscated and still controls a large part of U.S. territory. In 1933 Congress authorized the Tennessee Valley Authority, which flooded about 600,000 acres of land, in the interest of flood control. Critics have pointed out the irony of a flood-control program that permanently inundated far more acres than natural flooding had ever done. In total, the federal government owns about 650 million acres, or 28 percent, of the land of the United States. This includes a majority of the territory of some Western states: 89 percent of Alaska, 86 percent of Nevada, and 47 percent of California. Some of this land was U.S. territory never sold off to private owners or given to the states, but some of it was acquired through confiscation under the theory of eminent domain that makes the state the ultimate owner of all property. However acquired, federal lands, withdrawn from the market and managed for such purposes as conservation, flood control, timber production, recreation, and hydroelectric power, are no less socially owned than the mines and utilities nationalized by Britain, France, and Mexico.

THE FAILURE OF NATIONALIZATION
Clement Atlee's postwar government in Britain was the most effective socialist administration of the twentieth century. Winston Churchill, when he returned to power in 1951, did not touch most of the nationalized industries, though he did denationalize the iron and steel industry and the road transport of goods. Iron and steel were, however, renationalized in 1967. Subsequent Conservative governments did little to dismantle the system that had been put in place, until the election of Margaret Thatcher in 1979. Like her Liberal father, Thatcher had, under the influence of Keith Joseph and Alfred Sherman, become an economic liberal (in the European sense) who opposed government intervention in the economy and was determined to break the power the trade unions had over the British government. She also favored privatization of national industries, and in her first term she sold off the National Freight Company.

Labour Party leader Michael Foot, in facing the election of 1983, arranged for a party manifesto that called for renewed nationalization, along with nuclear disarmament and withdrawal from the European Economic Community. Described as "the longest suicide note in history," the party manifesto contributed to Thatcher's victory and spelled the end of nationalization. Thatcher promptly privatized the utility companies, selling shares to ordinary citizens. Other national companies met with a similar fate, though it was not until 1994 that the coal industry was fully privatized.

France had enacted a program of nationalization as massive as Britain's, but shortly after his election as prime minister, Jacques Chirac proposed an ambitious plan for privatizing sixty-five companies in five years. Opposed by the socialist president, Chirac had to compromise by preventing foreign acquisition of French companies and by reducing the size and speed of his project. Even so, twenty-nine businesses had been privatized by 1988, and the project has since been carried out by both socialist and nonsocialist governments.

Germany began privatizing companies in the former DDR (communist East Germany) shortly after reunification (1989), and Italy (in 1993) began selling off state-owned businesses, sometimes to foreign firms, a move that horrified some Italian conservatives. Privatization experiments in corrupt political systems, Mexico, Brazil, and post-communist Russia, have usually meant the transfer of enormous wealth from the public sector to an often criminal elite class. Critics have also claimed that privatization leads to unemployment and higher prices for services, but nationalized industries (e.g., British Rail) had been even more sharply criticized for poor service and indifference to the needs of the public.

PLANNING AND MODERNIZATION

Basic socialist economic objectives, such as full employment, egalitarian wage scales, and state ownership of major industries, presuppose a higher level of government regulation and planning than had been required in liberal states that rely upon the free market. In classical liberal theory, levels of production as well as wages and prices were not set by an agency; they resulted from the constant interplay of market forces. This understanding was framed in terms of economic laws; for example, the law of supply and demand, which says the greater the demand for a product or service, the higher will be the price of the product or wages to the laborer providing the service. In socialist theory, however, wages and prices, instead of being set by the market, were established on the basis of justice as determined by the officials in charge of making such decisions. The market, in other words, was replaced by agencies and planning boards. Socialists believed that they possessed an economic science that was up to the job, but liberal critics (such as Friedrich Hayek in *The Road to Serfdom*) argued that no person or group of people could ever possess sufficient information to second-guess the market. The result, liberals insisted, would be inefficiency and injustice. Why, they asked, should government officials decide who wins and who loses in economic competition?

Early socialists had not given much thought to managing a government because they believed that the history of class conflict would inevitably culminate in a socialist or communist state that would automatically do the right thing, either because the people would act justly or at least in their own best interest (as Marx and Engels seemed to believe) or because socialist intellectuals would make wise and disinterested decisions (as the Fabians thought). But neither Marx nor the Fabians had much practical experience in managing a business, much less in running a government. Socialist governments were faced with many economic problems, many of them (e.g., international economic crises, rising oil prices) beyond their control, but they also had to make good on their basic promises to increase wages and pensions and to improve welfare benefits. Such increases are not only costly, they are inflationary.

In simple terms, inflation means a continuous rise in prices and wages and a corresponding decrease in the value of money. There are many causes of inflation: Governments sometimes decrease the amount of gold or silver in their coinage, or, on the other hand, a large increase in the amount of precious metal in circulation can lower its value. When paper money is issued, it is easy enough to print more whenever the government needs it, but the market quickly responds by discounting the money and raising prices.

Socialist governments, then, had to find a way to increase wages and social spending without causing an inflationary spiral. According to a free-market economic theory known as monetarism, the task is impossible. The more a government spends, the more money it prints, and the less valuable the money becomes. Prices and wages rise in a dizzying upward spiral until people, losing confidence, begin to hoard not only precious metals but also basic commodities like food. The result, if the process is not checked, can be the sort of panic that in Weimar Germany made the Nazi takeover possible.

There was an alternative theory, however, authored by a British Liberal, John Maynard Keynes. Keynes believed that government spending, if properly managed, would stimulate the private sectors of the economy. By hiring the unemployed for public works projects, the government pays salaries that would be spent on manufactured goods. Manufacturing and mining companies would then increase production and hire more employees who would buy more goods and services. In Britain Keynesianism was institutionalized and managed, beginning in the mid–1960s, by such agencies as the Department of Economic Affairs, the National Board for Prices and Incomes, and the Industrial Reorganization Corporation.

In Sweden similar policies were advocated by the "Stockholm School" of economic thought in the 1930s. In the 1950s Swedish planners adopted a model produced by two trade union economists, Gösta Rehn and Rudolf Meidner. This Rehn-Meidner model set the overall objective of full employment but with the provisions that Sweden control inflation, continue its policies of social equality and cooperative control over wages to be exercised by strong unions, business representatives, and government, and use efficient central economic planning to ensure growth and productivity. This model (which echoes Marx's labor theory of value) required an enormous effort, since industries had to be thoroughly researched to determine wage standards that were "fair" but did not hinder growth or contribute to inflation. The difficulty of the task was complicated by the fact that Sweden, even though it adopted the goal of combating inflation, never fully abandoned Keynesian economic theory, which encouraged deficit spending.

Many politicians in Britain, France, and the United States became more or less pure Keynesians. Germans, even within the Social Democratic Party, were somewhat more cautious. Remembering that the disastrous inflation rates of the 1920s had contributed to Hitler's rise, the German central bank insisted on policies to curb inflation. This decision, while it slowed the growth of the German welfare state, may also have contributed to Germany's economic success. Later, as German unions demanded higher wages, shorter work weeks, longer vacations, and more welfare benefits, Germany faced some of the UK's economic woes that had given rise to the phrase, "the British disease": government debt, inflation, and lowered productivity.

Keynes was reassuring to all sides. He encouraged socialists to spend money on their programs, and, at the same time, he reassured capitalists that with proper management, the capitalist system could be preserved. Thus, socialists, capitalists, and even conservatives came increasingly to rely on Keynesian theory to justify the development of welfare states. In Britain, Conservatives and Labourites both advocated welfare state policies, but it was the Labourites who, with their talk of scientific management, persuaded the voters they could do the job and avoid the labor strikes that periodically crippled the economy.

THE YUGOSLAV "MIRACLE"

Keynesian theory *appears* to work in periods of economic expansion, but it also encouraged welfare-state governments to seek loans and, even more dangerously, to print money as they needed it. Yugoslavia seemed to flourish in the 1960s and 1970s, but the Yugoslav "miracle" was partly financed by loans from the World Bank and assistance from the U.S. government, which wanted to keep Yugoslavia detached from its former ally, the U.S.S.R. With the end of the Cold War, support dried up and there were debts to be paid. Part, at least, of the Yugoslav débacle in the 1990s can be traced to the optimistic economic planning of previous decades.

Postwar Yugoslavia was technically a nonaligned communist state, but, although the government initially introduced many Soviet-style measures—nationalization of industries, "Five Year Plans" to build up industry, special prisons for political dissidents, and strict control of the press—Marxist experimentation was rarely tried on the scale of the U.S.S.R. or the East European countries it controlled after the war. Expelled from the Cominform (the reinvented Comintern) in 1948 and cut off from 50 percent of its trade income, Yugoslavia was forced to pursue an independent path of development.

In the first few years after the war, Yugoslavia imitated the Soviet system, confiscating industries and businesses and trying (though failing abysmally) to lure the independent-minded peasants onto collective farms. After the split with the U.S.S.R. permanently isolated Yugoslavia from the Soviet bloc, Tito and his advisors gave up their attempt to collectivize farming and turned away from the central planning of industry in order to develop a less centralized model of "worker self-management."

To understand how this model worked, one has to know a little about the complex problems of the Yugoslav state. Yugoslavia had been established after World War I as a federated kingdom of Serbs, Croats, and Slovenes. The King of Serbia, whose troops had fought to liberate the

Balkans from Austrian and Turkish rule, became king of the new state. In addition to the three main national groups, there were also sizable groups of Slavic Muslims (in Bosnia, and Albanians in Montenegro and as a majority in the part of Serbia known as Kosovo-Metohija). Vojvodina, which stretches between Belgrade and the Hungarian border, was home to significant numbers of Hungarians, Slovaks, and Germans, though Germans were expelled at the end of World War II. From the day of its establishment, Yugoslavia was plagued by the separatist and regionalist movements that tore it to pieces in the 1990s.

Although ethnic patriotism was forbidden by Tito, each republic was out for as much as it could get. Croatia and Slovenia, for example, were the most industrialized republics, and they resented the investments made in less-developed regions. Serbs, however, made up the largest ethnic group, and they felt that their interests were neglected and their sacrifices in fighting Austria-Hungary in World War I and Germany in World War II (when Croatia was an ally of the Third Reich) were being ignored by Tito, who was half-Croatian and half-Slovenian. One partial solution to these rivalries was to decentralize industrial management. Under the new system adopted after the split with the U.S.S.R., industry was managed by workers' councils under the direction of the separate republics (e.g., Serbia, Croatia, Slovenia) or local governments. Only transportation and the postal service were under direct control of the Yugoslav federal government. In the early years, U.S. aid was of considerable help, and it was replaced by a series of "soft" (on easy terms) development loans from the United States and billions of dollars of World Bank loans in the 1960s.

The effect of so much foreign investment was dramatic. Production and exports increased rapidly, though not productivity. The Yugoslav "miracle" was held up as proof that an economy could grow as quickly under socialism as under capitalism. But aid, as it so often does, had distorting effects. Yugoslavia had formerly had a fairly prosperous agricultural economy, but with Western assistance the communist leadership was able to persist in neglecting agriculture and developing heavy industry, even when it was unprofitable. Some of the economic decisions made were purely political, often at the behest of a local political boss. For example, an aluminum plant was built near Podgorica, the capital of Montenegro, even though there was neither aluminum nor coal nearby. Although a great eyesore and a tremendous source of environmental pollution, the plant never turned a profit.

Management by workers' councils proved more effective than centralized planning, but it was far less efficient than capitalist management and encouraged a contempt for expertise. With the increase of prosperity, there was a rising expectation of economic freedom, but the old-guard leadership could not so much as dream of privatizing state-owned industries. Ironically, it was the independent farmers who were able to take the best advantage of economic and banking reforms put in place in 1965; the managers of state industries seemed to lack the entrepreneurial ambition required to turn a profit.

By the 1970s and 1980s the economy was becoming stagnant, and the interest on the $20 billion foreign debt, which was becoming an increasingly significant burden, had to be rescheduled. Unemployment rose above 15 percent, while real earnings fell. By the end of the 1980s the annual inflation rate had risen to 2,600 percent. After Tito's death and the disintegration of the Soviet empire, Yugoslavia, whose comparative prosperity had been the envy of Eastern Europe, descended quickly into poverty, chaos, and war.

Yugoslavia is only one of many similar casualties of international philanthropy. Many others can be cited both from Eastern Europe and the Third World, and industrialized Western Europe is hardly exempt. Britain, after World War II, also expected to finance an expanding welfare state with U.S. loans. The United States had been very generous during the war, but with victory there came a revulsion in the American electorate against high taxes and foreign aid expenditures. In ending the Lend Lease agreement, which had helped to finance Britain's war effort, the United States left her ally nearly bankrupt at the very time when she was embarking on an ambitious project of reconstruction and socialization.

Socialists do not regard international economic assistance as charity, which is given freely out of an abundance and from motives of pity. Global philanthropy, by contrast, is mandated by principles of justice, and it should not matter if the givers do not feel pity for the recipients or even if the givers find themselves in straitened circumstances, so long as there is a significant gap in wealth, as there certainly is between Western European countries and the Third World. Thus, even as Britain and the Scandinavian countries were suffering economic hard times in the 1970s, they were contributing generously to international relief efforts.

FREE MARKET LIBERALISM'S PYRRHIC VICTORY

Middle-class voters in Europe and North America had learned to enjoy many benefits of the welfare state, but increasingly strident calls for economic justice—that is, higher taxes and more income redistribution—were scarcely attractive to people who were already feeling the pinch of several decades of socialism. Since the 1940s socialist parties had presented themselves as having the technical expertise to avoid labor unrest. This meant a close collaboration of trade unions and government. Far from content with their enhanced political power, major unions in Britain, France, and Italy were emboldened to demand more, and they were not afraid to call strikes against socialist parties.

In the 1960s and 1970s, the British Labour Party leader Harold Wilson (prime minister in 1964–1970, 1974–1976) tried to broaden his party's appeal by putting a new emphasis on technological modernization. The modernization process was to be presided over by a new Ministry of Technology and a Department for Economic Affairs that implemented Wilson's Keynesian economic views. For one reason or another, Wilson's programs failed to stimulate the economy. This failure, combined with the strident leftism of his successors, made the Conservative Party's victory in 1979 possible.

The Labourites did not shift gears, however, and technological modernization also became the justification for a new wave of nationalization and centralized economic planning, which party leaders proposed as a response to Thatcher's successful campaign to privatize those sectors of the economy that had been nationalized. The manifest failure of nationalized industries, combined with the persistent rhetoric of economic revolution, ensured an unprecedented term in office for Thatcher—nearly eleven continuous years.

Thatcher's administration was often described as revolutionary, and in terms of applied economic theory, it probably was. Keynesianism, and the deficit spending that accompanies Keynesian policies, had been the reigning economic theory of the technocrats in Europe and the United States who constructed the welfare state, but the economic crises of the 1970s—inflation, stagnant growth, unemployment—gave credence to the classical liberal arguments against deficit spending and central planning. The 1980s witnessed a virtual free-market revolution in Britain (Thatcher), France (Chirac), Germany (Helmut

Kohl), and the United States (Ronald Reagan), though the size and scope of government was barely dented, especially in the United States, conservatives could only boast of slowing the growth of government spending. Thatcher had greater impact on the UK's economy, but no major liberal or conservative party had any major success in slowing, much less reversing, the moral and social revolution that had taken place.

The Liberal opponents of socialism, however, had accomplished one thing. For the time being they had squelched the dream of a socially controlled economic system. Even when socialist and left-liberal parties returned to power in Britain, Germany, and the United States, they had learned their lesson and adopted neoliberal platforms that preserved and expanded welfare programs, but with fiscal control and some respect for the free market.

By the time of Bill Clinton's election as U.S. president in 1992 and Tony Blair's election as British prime minister in 1997, the leaders of the Democratic Party and Labour Party (like their counterparts in Germany and France) had come to accept the proposition that the market should be allowed to operate within more or less strict limits. This did not mean they were any the less committed to continuing their welfare state policies. On the contrary, they were determined to allow the private economy to function and to manage their welfare programs with greater efficiency. In Britain, the United States, and Germany, large numbers of middle-class voters accepted the neoliberal arguments made by Blair, Clinton, and Chancellor Gerhard Schroeder. Tony Blair's "New Labour," in economic terms, was nearly as liberal-capitalist as any British government since the 1920s. At the end of the day, it was Thatcher's and Reagan's fiscal policies that triumphed, but classical liberals had no cause for jubilation, since many of the socialist goals—state-provided pensions and health care, central management, and equal opportunity—were now endorsed by most parties on both left and right.

4
Pursuing Equality ■ ■ ■

IN THE YEARS FOLLOWING WORLD WAR II, the states of Western Europe rapidly attained many of the major goals that had been advocated by the socialists of the Second International. Governments were elected democratically by the vote of all male citizens and eventually, after Switzerland (in 1971) became the last European country to grant women the vote, both male and female citizens. Programs of social insurance and national health care were being established. The eight-hour workday had been adopted; unions were not only legal but played an active role in the political process; and in Britain, France, and Italy (to say nothing of Eastern Europe and Russia) governments were nationalizing large-scale industries.

In Germany, the Netherlands, and Scandinavia, however, socialists pursued somewhat different strategies. Instead of nationalizing utilities and industries, these countries preferred to create systems of wealth-transfer through taxation, cradle-to-grave welfare, and control of the economy by means of formal collaboration among the leaders of government, business, and labor. These approaches were also adopted, to one degree or another, by other countries embarked on the socialist path of development.

EQUALITY THROUGH TAXATION: THE SWEDISH MODEL
Socialism (in its social democratic form) was introduced to Swedish politics in the early 1880s, and in the 1920s the social democratic leader

In 1971, Switzerland became the last European country to give women the right to vote. The equality of women, although an issue unrelated to the main goals of socialism, was advocated by Plato, Marx, and most modern socialist movements.

Hjalmar Brantling served three times as prime minister. In the 1930s the Social Democratic Party of Sweden (SAP), since it was frequently in coalition with liberal parties, did not propose any sweeping programs of political restructuring, though it did introduce programs to provide housing, employment, and pensions. Even in 1932 when the SAP received a majority, party leaders talked about economic growth and dropped even the word *socialism* from their platform. The most important step was the Saltsjöbaden Agreement (1938), which set up a system of active collaboration between unions and businesses with the primary purpose of collective bargaining to avoid strikes. Similar arrangements were made in Denmark and Norway.

Graduated taxation, that is, a program that assesses higher incomes at higher tax rates, is a common method used by socialist governments to redistribute income. In 1891 German Socialists adopted the radical Erfurt Program, calling for a massive welfare state to be financed by graduated taxation. The program was quickly imitated by other socialist parties, including Sweden's SAP. After the end of World War II, the SAP was in power continuously until the 1970s. Working with its allies (particularly the Farmers Party), the party introduced a steeply graduated income tax that has been described by critics as "punitive." Average tax rates in the 1970s and 1980s reached 65 percent to 75 percent.

One way of looking at taxation is to examine the ratio between taxpayers receiving income from the free market and tax-receivers (people on welfare or employed by government). The proportion of tax-receivers to market-earners in Sweden rose from 0.4 in 1960 to 1.8 in 1995. In other words, by 1995 there were nearly twice as many people receiving their income from the government as there were in the private sector.

Another means of reducing inequality was to tax both the profits of a firm and the personal capital gains of the owners. This could raise an individual's tax rate to astronomical heights, approaching or even exceeding 100 percent. The height of absurdity was reached in 1976, when Sweden's most famous citizen, film director Ingmar Bergman, was arrested on charges of tax evasion. The case was complex, involving the director's corporate as well as personal earnings. The bottom line was that Bergman was being taxed at a rate of 139 percent. Three years later the filmmaker was exonerated and paid only a tiny fraction of the original demand, while the government had to pay the court costs of $500,000. Although the case contributed to the electoral defeat of the SAP, Sweden's most important modern artist is still commonly regarded, nearly fifty years later, as an unpatriotic tax cheat.

Sweden's tax system was only the most extreme version of a general phenomenon. When Margaret Thatcher took office in 1979, Britain's top income tax rate was 83 percent and the basic rate was 33 percent. During that same period, the top U.S. rate was 70 percent, which President Reagan lowered to 28 percent. The federal income tax had been introduced by Abraham Lincoln but was eventually declared illegal on the grounds that the Constitution forbids the federal government to levy any capitation tax (that is, a tax against personal income or wealth) except as determined by Article One of the Constitution. In 1913, however, the taxation of incomes was made legal by the Sixteenth Amendment.

Income-tax rates have risen and fallen. The top rate in the World War I era was 70 percent, which was cut to 25 percent in the 1920s, but, by the time of John F. Kennedy's election as president (1960), it had risen to a rate of 90 percent, which Kennedy lowered to 70 percent as part of a successful plan to stimulate the economy. Critics of the graduated income tax say that it punishes productivity and success, because the more income a person makes, the higher the rate at which he or she pays taxes. Supporters say it is only simple fairness to require the rich to pay a higher percentage of their income. Of course, the rich do not always pay at a higher rate. The U.S. tax code, drawn up and revised under the influence of many different pressure groups, contains many loopholes that only the rich are able to take advantage of.

Inheritance taxes are another popular method for redistributing income through taxation. Sweden, Britain, and the United States (in 1916) introduced graduated inheritance taxes. In the midst of the Great Depression, Congress raised the top rate on estates worth $50 million (nearly $700 million in today's terms) or more, to 70 percent. Though Sweden eventually eliminated inheritance taxes, the issue is still a source of political controversy in the United States.

SOCIAL INSURANCE

At the first meeting of the Second International in Paris on the centenary of the French Revolution (1889), socialists demanded the emancipation of workers and the abolition of wage-slavery, and they also called for the creation of a society in which women and men of all nations would enjoy the wealth produced by the workers.

Specifically, they wanted to abolish child labor and establish the principle of equal pay for equal work for women.

These were bold ideas, and even one hundred years later, despite a dramatic move in their direction, no society could be said to have carried them out completely. Nonetheless, even before 1889, many European states had enacted some socialistic policies. Germany led the way. Although the German government had enacted antisocialist legislation that forced socialist leaders into exile, less than ten years later (in 1889), Kaiser Wilhelm I informed his parliament that workers who had been disabled because of old age or illness deserved to be cared for by the state. This letter, as well as the social insurance plan that was drawn up, was the work of German Chancellor Otto von Bismarck (chancellor 1862–1890). Germany's new pension system, unlike the British plan adopted in 1911, was funded by contributions from the workers, and, unlike the American social security system, it was designed to work on a sound actuarial basis, that is, like a for-profit insurance company, which in the long run takes in at least as much money as it pays out. Bismarck was careful to restrict the payment of pensions to people age sixty-five and up—roughly the life expectancy of the average German at the time. In the 1880s Germany also introduced accident and health insurance plans, though not on the generous basis of post-World War II systems.

Bismarck had several reasons for establishing social insurance. He was no doubt motivated by a humane concern for workers who could no longer rely on the old protections that had formerly been provided by extended families and small villages. On a more practical level, the "Iron Chancellor" wished to take the wind out of the sails of socialists and other leftists who were calling for more extreme measures. This is a pattern that repeats itself throughout most of the twentieth century: Conservative governments, to win votes, either initiate socialist legislation or else consolidate innovations introduced by socialists.

In 1913 Sweden's liberal government (through the National Pension Act) took the further step of setting up the first compulsory pension plan that applied to every citizen. Even in the nineteenth century, however, Sweden's liberal government had passed poor relief laws. Between the two world wars, most governments of Western Europe and North America had set up some kind of pension program. In Sweden, the SAP, which was solidly in power between 1932 and 1938, not only established the eight-hour work day but began the construction of the most thoroughgoing welfare state in Europe. As early as the 1930s, the Swedish system included pensions indexed for inflation, maternity leave for employed mothers, a housing benefit aimed at large families, paid vacations, and government loans to newlyweds.

Britain took its first steps toward creating a welfare system under Liberal Party leadership. Rent control (which supposedly keeps housing affordable but almost always reduces the amount of housing for rent) was enacted during World War I in 1915, and a local housing program, designed to provide decent and affordable working-class housing was initiated in 1919. In December 1942, Sir William Beveridge, a Liberal who had gone to Germany in 1907 to study social insurance, proposed that all people of working age should make a weekly contribution to an insurance system. The system, in return, would pay benefits to people who were sick, unemployed, retired, or widowed. Beveridge argued that his plan would provide a minimum standard of living "below which no one should be allowed to fall." These measures were adopted by Atlee's Labour government as the 1946 National Insurance Act, which provided pensions to all British citizens.

In the United States, Social Security was adopted in 1935 as part of President Franklin Delano Roosevelt's New Deal. By that time, twenty countries around the world, from Argentina to Tasmania, had adopted some form of state pension. In the United States, few companies had comprehensive pension systems, and although thirty states had set up pensions, they covered only a tiny fraction of the elderly. Most older Americans either relied on personal savings or were taken care of by relatives. However, the Depression badly affected both sources of support: many banks had failed, depriving the depositors of their savings. Under the circumstances, parents could not necessarily rely on their unemployed and impoverished children. Americans faced an additional problem in that their habit of moving around tended to separate families.

The Social Security Act, which was signed into law by Roosevelt, covered workers in commerce and industry. The Federal Insurance Contribution Act (1937) provided for workers' income to be taxed to support the system. In 1939, coverage was extended to families and in 1950 applied to workers outside commerce and industry. In 1972, it was indexed for inflation, meaning that benefits were increased at a rate intended to keep up with inflation (the decreasing value of the dollar), though in practice the indexing has outpaced inflation.

The New Deal

Elected during the Great Depression, President Franklin Delano Roosevelt borrowed the slogan "The New Deal" from the democratic socialist Stuart Chase. Although in the 1932 election Roosevelt had campaigned on a program of cutting government spending and government interference in business, the New Deal proved to be a sweeping and controversial program of social reconstruction and centralized planning, including an agricultural support program, social security, the Tennessee Valley Authority, and the National Recovery Administration (NRA). When the NRA was declared unconstitutional by the Supreme Court, the president planned to increase the number of justices—a procedure known as "packing the court"—but he was prevented by Congress. A second phase of the New Deal, initiated in 1935, was even more controversial because it seemed to favor the poorer classes at the expense of the well-to-do. Although Roosevelt and his supporters claimed that his policies ended the Depression, critics have claimed that the New Deal prolonged and aggravated the Depression, which was brought to an end by World War II. Whichever side is correct, most of the New Deal has become a permanent part of the U.S. government.

Although social security has been generally popular, it is not without its problems. The most serious of them is the fact that it is not truly an insurance system, and there is no actual social security fund from which claims are paid. Payments to the government under the Federal Insurance Contribution Act are more like taxes than contributions to an individual retirement account. This is because currently employed taxpayers are not paying for their own retirement but are being assessed to support retirees. Finally, the system has been so broadened as to include people who have never worked or paid into it. The result is an actuarially unsound arrangement that faces bankruptcy. Although more money comes in than is paid out (the 2005 surplus was about $88 billion), the balance will begin to shift as the Baby Boomers (Americans born between the end of World War II and the election of President Lyndon Johnson in 1964) retire.

By 2018, it is predicted, outgoing payments will exceed income. There is no actual reserve fund to cover the deficit, since the social security fund has been borrowed from to pay other government expenses. In fact, the debt to social security is several times greater than the official national debt. Some have compared social security to a classic Ponzi scheme or pyramid, which depends on an ever-increasing pool of new contributors to pay off the older class of dupes. Few critics, however, challenge the basic socialist principle that it is government's responsibility, by one method or another, to provide retirement income.

Critics also argue that social security has the further disadvantage of making Americans dependent on the federal government. Some have recommended adoption of something like the new Chilean system, which in effect requires workers to invest 10 percent of their before-tax income into a retirement savings account, which, like any investment portfolio, can increase in value.

HEALTH CARE, DISABILITY, VACATIONS

Along with old-age pensions, socialized medicine is one of the most important welfare programs adopted by socialist states. Before the twentieth century, most people either paid for their own medical care or asked for charity. In completely socialized systems, however, medical care is, in theory, the responsibility of the entire nation, and no one, rich or poor, can be denied assistance. In Germany, Bismarck had set up a compulsory health insurance system as a parallel to his pension program, but the new system failed to lower health-care costs; instead, it increased them. This was an ominous development.

The British system of socialized medicine is perhaps the best known. The Labour government that came to power in 1945, in addition to nationalizing industries and establishing a comprehensive pension plan, also enacted a wide range of social programs. The minimum age at which students could leave school was raised to fifteen, a vast system of public housing was begun, and major steps toward a "cradle to grave" welfare state were made by health minister Aneurin Bevan, the most radical socialist in the cabinet. To this day members of the Labour Party continue to regard the creation (in 1948) of Britain's tax-funded National Health Service as the party's most significant accomplishment.

Before changes were introduced by Margaret Thatcher in the 1980s, Britain's National Health Service (NHS) offered free medical care to everyone in the UK. Patients were charged nothing, and the system was paid for by taxation. Local governments were in charge of health clinics, but most general practitioners and specialists were private, though they were paid by the government on a per-patient basis. Rising costs eventually forced the government to charge a small copayment for dental care and prescription medicines. Such reforms did not make the system solvent. The NHS has gone through several reorganizations, but it is increasingly apparent that the system cannot keep up with the burden of an aging population.

Most developed countries have some form of publicly funded health care. In some, the system is supported by general revenues; in others, special tax funds are set up for this purpose. Some countries, such as Canada, pay 100 percent of a patient's expenses, while others pay only a percentage. In Sweden the publicly funded medical system was set up to be universal (available for all), comprehensive (covering all medical expenses), and compulsory (no one can opt out). Physician and hospital services take a small patient fee, but their services are funded through the taxation scheme administered by local government entities. Both Germany and Sweden offer unlimited universal coverage. This means that the government pays for visits to the doctor, hospitalization, and pharmaceutical products with very low deductibles.

Closely related to medical insurance are government programs to provide income to workers disabled by injury or disease. Disability payments in the United States, which run between 18 percent and 63 percent of the average wage and last no longer than fifty-two weeks, are well behind what is offered in Germany: 70 percent of gross earnings for up to seventy-eight weeks. Sweden is even more generous, paying 80 percent of gross earnings for an indefinite period of time. Similarly, most socialist countries have guaranteed minimum vacations—the European average is four weeks a year. The United States, by contrast, has no guaranteed vacation, though some private employers do grant several weeks or even a month; two weeks is standard.

Health-care systems, like other aspects of the welfare state, have been in flux since the 1980s. By the 1990s many European governments began reexamining their socialized health-care systems. The systems were costly and cumbersome, critics alleged. Patients in the UK, when surveyed in opinion polls, are far more likely than Americans to complain of long waiting periods. Worse, Britain's expensive system has not kept up with medical technology. Even technology pioneered in the UK is less available there than in the United States. Sweden, in the late 1990s, ran a series of experiments with privatization, and they found that doctors' visits were actually more expensive in the government system. With deregulation and privatization, both costs and waiting times decreased significantly.

Rather more serious charges have been made against the Dutch health service. The high cost of the system has encouraged both doctors and patients' relatives to apply cost-benefit analysis to elderly patients, it is alleged. Termination of life support, in such cases, saves the government money and provides a more speedy settlement of the patient's estate. Critics have not shrunk from describing this as a state program of euthanasia.

In the United States, by contrast, people still rely on private practitioners whom they pay, usually, through rather costly insurance plans. Retired Americans rely on Medicare, and the poor turn to Medicaid. The U.S. system, however, is also undergoing considerable stress, as the price of health care is increasingly under the control of large medical insurance providers, and the United States seems almost irresistibly drawn toward a universal, government-controlled health care system.

BROADENING THE AGENDA

By the end of the 1960s, most Western European countries (e.g., Britain, France, Sweden, Denmark, Germany, The Netherlands, Austria, and the UK) had developed a wide array of socialist programs that can fairly be described as cradle-to-grave welfare states. However, fulfillment of early promises meant rising expectations, and European and American leftists began to speak of more fundamental social changes aimed at traditional sex roles and at turning over more and more family functions to the state. In *Inequality*, a highly influential book of the early 1970s, the American leftist Christopher Jenks conceded that government educational programs had little success in reducing inequality, because the most significant indicator of a child's future success was not the amount of money spent on his schooling but the quality of his family background. Families in which habits of diligence, thrift, self-control, and academic study were inculcated typically produced children who did well in school and went on to successful careers. Exceptions abound, but policies are based not on exceptions but on general statistical trends.

Jenks was hardly the first leftist to understand the significance of the family in generating inequalities, and both communist and socialist governments made a variety of efforts to equalize opportunities by intervening in family life. In the United States, the best-known programs include publicly funded education, programs to equalize school district incomes, Head Start, and college loans for the economically disadvantaged.

In the UK, Labour Party leader Harold Wilson hoped to reduce inequality by means of what he called the "Social Contract," and in "Labour's Programme 1973," the party promised to bring about a "fundamental and irreversible shift in the balance of power and wealth in favor of working people and their families." The implications of the program were serious and might have sent Britain down the road of other Marxist states that have socialized the family, but Britain's sluggish economy gave few opportunities for expanding government expenditures. Nonetheless, Labour Party governments did introduce a child benefit allowance to parents or guardians in addition to a system of "redundancy pay," that is, a kind of unemployment compensation for workers whose specialty or line of work is no longer in demand. The institution of the family, however, was not directly attacked.

SOCIALIZING THE FAMILY

Since the early nineteenth century, the family has been seen as the final frontier for socialism. Even by the time of the French Revolution, some utopian socialists and sexual libertines argued that the family had outlived whatever useful functions it might have possessed. Marx and Engels went further, lumping the family together with private property and the state as instruments of oppression. In the twentieth century Sigmund Freud (the founder of psychoanalysis) and his disciples have often portrayed the family as the institution that nurtured neurosis and sexual dysfunction. Feminists, on the other hand, complained that the sexual division of labor, by which men were workers and women were domestic caregivers, had imprisoned all women, but especially working-class women.

As social and political radicals, nineteenth century communists were accused of advocating—and practicing—"free love." Both charges contained a good deal of truth, as they did in later radical movements (e.g., in the 1960s). However, some revolutionary leaders learned that sexual freedom, while it certainly undermined the bourgeois order, also destabilized revolutionary movements and made considerable trouble for the architects of a new communist order. The Yugoslav communist Milovan Djilas was known for his puritanical disapproval of communist playboys.

The disagreement between libertines and puritans surfaced in the early years of the U.S.S.R. when the Marxist-feminist Alexandra Kollontai argued that traditional marriage and the autonomous family were obstacles to the progress of the revolutionary state. Already in noncommunist Europe, she pointed out, state subsidies for maternity and child-rearing were a first step toward the ultimate goal: "The transfer of the task of caring for the new generation, so precious to mankind, from the shoulders of private, individual parents to the whole community."

According to Kollontai, secular marriage and liberalized divorce were destroying "the essential basis of the social stability of the bourgeoisie . . . the monogamous, property-orientated family." Although she was rarely bold enough to hold up free love as an ideal, her advocacy of female equality in all spheres of life was an implicit argument for sexual freedom. Lenin became uneasy with Kollontai. Although as a Marxist he advocated erotic freedom in principle, he did not want to encourage any social revolution that threatened to destabilize the power structure of the dictatorship he had worked so hard to establish. In the end, Lenin and his successor, Stalin, contented themselves with destroying the power of extended families. In the U.S.S.R. the nuclear family was expected to carry out the basic functions of nursing, feeding, and clothing children, and preparing them for the state institutions that would fit them out to be citizens of a socialist state.

Feminism and socialism are not necessarily related movements. In Europe, between the two world wars, a variety of feminist movements sprang up; some were related to agrarian and back-to-the-farm movements; others were socialist, fascist, or even National Socialist. In America it was the businessmen of the Republican Party who first proposed an equal rights amendment, following the logic that families with two workers (man and wife) would help to keep wages low. However, feminism is significant for the development of socialism when it helps to establish policies that turn over traditional family functions (e.g., education, child care, and child protection) to state agencies.

Kollontai was forced to become a diplomat, which in her case was another word for exile. Rejected in the Soviet Union, her ideas had more impact in the West, though she anticipated by several decades the feminist thought of Simone de Beauvoir, Kate Millet, and Betty Friedan. However, as early as the 1920s Alva Myrdal, a young Swedish socialist, called for "collectivized homes" where husbands and wives would both work outside the home, while meals would be prepared and served in group dining halls, and children would be cared for by professional day care workers. This, she believed, would reverse the slide in Swedish fertility rates. During the 1930s, she and her husband Gunnar developed the concept to include aggressive sex education for all children, legal contraception, and abortion to liberate women from childbearing, universal health care, and massive state subsidies to those who had children.

The Myrdals' career typifies the contradictions and changes within the socialist movement. Trained as an economist, Gunnar Myrdal encouraged the development of Keynesian economic policies in Sweden. He and his wife Alva were seriously concerned with the decline in Swedish birth rates, and their family policies were designed to encourage population increase. Gunnar also contributed to the American political debate with his book *The American Dilemma*, in which he condemned the United States for failing to improve opportunities for African Americans. But there is another side to their work. The Myrdals also favored eugenics (scientific human breeding) policies that were considered progressive in the 1930s, and the Swedish government set up a eugenics program that included sterilization and lobotomizing of the "unfit."

The Nobel Prize–winning economist Gunnar Myrdal was, with his wife Alva, an important influence on worldwide socialist politics after World War II.

The feminist concept of the family was not embraced by ordinary Swedes until the 1960s and 1970s, when Sweden became the Myrdals' dream come true. Divorce was immediately granted at the request of one spouse, and, as increasing numbers of women entered the workforce, children spent much of the time in collectivized daycares and schools. In 1987 laws were passed that reduced the legal obligations of marriage and put nonmarital consensual unions on more or less the same level as marriage. The same privilege was extended to same-sex unions in 1995.

Sweden, although it has been on the cutting edge of the sexual

Gunnar and Alva Myrdal

Alva and Gunnar Myrdal may be the most politically influential couple of the twentieth century. Both received a Nobel Prize, Gunnar the Prize in Economics (1974) and Alva the Peace Prize (1982). Gunnar, a trained economist, taught economics at Stockholm University (1933–1947) while serving simultaneously as a Social Democratic Party member of the Swedish parliament. He also served as minister for trade and was for ten years executive secretary of the UN Commission for Europe. As a democratic socialist, he worked to promote the ideal of the welfare state in Sweden and around the world. His published work includes influential studies of poverty and racism.

Alva Myrdal had an equally successful career as a social thinker and diplomat. Graduating from university in 1924, she married Gunnar and quickly became a partner in his work, in some areas the dominant partner. In the 1930s, as coauthor (with Gunnar) of *Crisis in the Population Question*, she became a leading voice in the movement to halt Sweden's demographic decline. She served her government as a member of parliament, as ambassador to India, and as delegate to the disarmament conference in Geneva. From 1950–1955 she headed UNESCO's social science section. The Myrdal legacy has been carried on by their son Jan, a Maoist who has written widely on China.

revolution, is hardly alone. Norway and Denmark, as well as many North European and North American countries, have enacted similar measures. By the 1980s most countries of the European Union (Britain excepted) guaranteed maternity leave and provided state-subsidized day care. France, for example, has both private and state-run nurseries and day-care programs for children as young as three months (three months being the average period for maternity leave). Public facilities are funded and directed by local governments that charge fees according to the means of the parents. In France as in Sweden, the expanding health care and welfare bureaucracy led to the creation of public-sector jobs, a majority of which went to women.

In Sweden one of the results, which should have been easy to anticipate, has been the decline of marriage as an institution. By the 1990s more children were born out of wedlock than within marriage. A similar trend was observed in other countries, such as the United States, where Aid to Families With Dependent Children, before it was dismantled by President Clinton, was blamed for encouraging sexual promiscuity and illegitimacy. Critics of such programs have argued repeatedly that government always gets what it pays for, and subsidies to illegitimacy inevitably increase the rate of illegitimate births. Defenders make the counterargument that women in poverty need government assistance and suggest that the only real problem is with the social stigma attached to illegitimacy.

Before the 1960s, socialist movements were reluctant to endorse what has come to be known as the sexual revolution, which can be roughly defined as the separation of sex and procreation by means of legalized contraception, abortion, and homosexuality, as well as sex education in the schools. By the end of that turbulent decade, however, these issues had received broad acceptance in socialist and leftist parties. Legalization was only the beginning. In Yugoslavia as in the Soviet bloc, contraceptives and abortions were both provided free of charge. In the UK both abortion and homosexuality were legalized in 1967.

Abortion became a cutting-edge issue for socialists. German leftists in 1974 passed a law legalizing abortion on demand, but conservatives had it declared unconstitutional two years later. Since abortion laws in Europe were passed by democratically elected parliaments, they reflect something like a majority consensus within each country. In some countries, such as Holland, abortion on demand has been permitted since 1981, while in others, waiting periods and counseling may be required and, in the case of minors, parental consent.

In the United States, in contrast to Europe, the broadest abortion rights were declared by the Supreme Court without a democratic debate. This has caused a violent rift in public opinion, lasting several decades, that makes abortion one of the most divisive issues in the United States. Still, abortion and gay rights have become almost articles of faith for the Democratic Party in the United States, and the equal rights platform has become so respectable that even the Republican Party finds it difficult to mount a united and coherent opposition.

SOCIALISM IN DISARRAY

By the end of the 1970s, socialist programs for wealth redistribution through taxation and welfare programs were in serious trouble, as rising expectations collided with the realities of inflation and high taxes. The "British disease" became something like a pandemic in western Europe. It was not long before calls for reform and retrenchment gained a sympathetic hearing from voters.

Sweden and Britain were among the countries most affected by economic stagnation. During the 1970s, Sweden continued to develop a cooperative system of economic planning that set "solidaristic" wages for all workers. These wages, considerably above the market level, were supposed to show social solidarity by equalizing the incomes of the citizens. By the 1990s a high-level manager was earning only about twice the salary of an ordinary worker. This might well be a just wage system, but it offers few incentives for hard work or ambition.

At the same time, Sweden virtually guaranteed full employment, not merely to the citizens generally but to workers in specific sectors of the economy. Thus, an economic turndown in the steel industry was not supposed to cause steelworkers to be laid off or fired. To prevent unemployment, ensure egalitarian wages, and encourage efficiency, increasingly aggressive labor unions collaborated with business and government. This tripartite system culminated in the Joint Consultation Act (1976), which had almost as much power to plan the economy as Soviet officials had under their Five Year Plans. This was the high water mark of Swedish social and economic planning, since middle-class dissatisfaction with high taxes and government meddling led to the Social Democratic Party's defeat in that very year.

The Swedish model had seemed to promise a U.S. standard of living cushioned by the guarantees of a socialist welfare state. It was emulated or paralleled by similar developments in Norway, Denmark, and Austria (among many others). The results have not been entirely encouraging. By the 1980s Sweden's tax burden was greater than any of its European competitors: In Sweden taxes represented 55.3 percent of the GNP compared with the UK's 37.4 percent and Switzerland's 32.5 percent.

Not surprisingly, Sweden's economy, from the late 1960s on, began to sag; by the late 1980s, inflation was running at twice the general European level, while growth and productivity in the 1970s and 1980s was stagnant. Government debt reached a high of 75 percent of the gross national product (a measure of a national population's entire income) in 1994, though by 2005 it had fallen to 52 percent. The improvements are largely the result of economic reforms and budget retrenchment, though Sweden in 2004 still had the highest overall tax burden in the world (about 50 percent), while Denmark had the honor of having the greatest income-tax pressure.

Sweden is not the only socialist country to have modified or reduced its system of economic management. Margaret Thatcher, in addition to the vigorous privatization plan she implemented, also made efforts to lighten the tax burden and reduce regulatory red tape and government interference in market activities. Faced with rising inflation (over 10 percent in 1979), Thatcher cut income-tax rates and increased the VAT (value-added tax, basically a national sales tax).

Though the Thatcher revolution eventually ran out of steam, it is unlikely that her Labour Party successors will return to the policies of Clement Atlee and Harold Wilson. It is significant that Prime Minister Blair, instead of desiring to "soak the rich," as the socialists used to say, claims he wants only to make everyone in Britain "stakeholders" in the society. This is basically what happened in the United States, where working-class people own their own homes and enjoy many of the advantages of the middle class. But, even as the socialist economic revolution was losing momentum, socialists and their leftist allies were discovering new issues—some of them half-forgotten pieces of earlier socialist programs—to use as the foundation for the next wave of an ever-expanding social revolution.

5
Expanding the Mission ■ ■ ■

COMPARED WITH ANARCHISM, REVOLUTIONARY COMMUNISM, or even free-market capitalism, democratic socialism may seem a drab political ideology that is dedicated to nothing more inspiring than old-age pensions, universal health care, and publicly owned utilities. Nonetheless, as an ideal it continues to attract committed followers. Part of the attraction may derive from socialism's revolutionary roots: Even the middle-class leaders of the British Labour Party have never completely given up the language of social revolution. Equally attractive to many converts is the moral message of socialism that asks men and women to live for something beyond the "getting and spending" that is the gospel of modern capitalism.

Like other radical movements, socialism has had to accommodate itself to changing circumstances. Each generation of socialists has found new outlets for the revolutionary impulse, and socialist parties in the mid-twentieth century, even as they were turning away from nationalization schemes, embraced feminism, sexual freedom, anti-colonialism, and minority rights, and by the end of the last century a typical socialist agenda might include protection of endangered species, same-sex marriage, Third World development, and global government. Here, we outline some of the major noneconomic issues that socialism has accumulated and show their relationship, when it exists, with the historic goals of socialist parties.

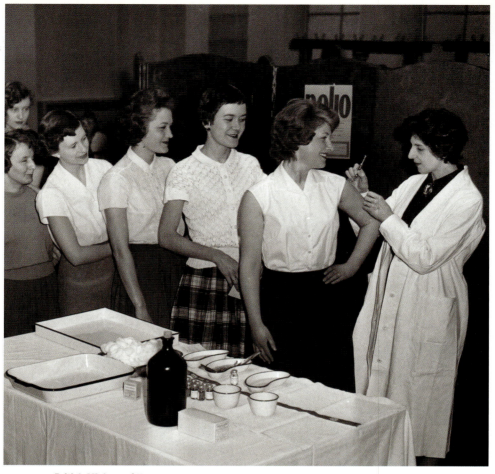

British Ministry of Health workers are photographed receiving vaccines advertising the importance of immunization. In the late 1940s, Britain established one of the first comprehensive systems of national health care.

AGAINST THE CHURCH

Socialism (and communism) began as a quasi-religious movement in the sense that it is supposed to explain and fulfill the purpose of human life. The very existence of God was anathema to Marx and some of his utopian-socialist predecessors, because such a being, lying outside of history and beyond the material human realm, would define the purpose of human life and deflect human aspirations away from socialism to itself. As August Comte argued, man could never establish a rational and secular society so long as individuals devoted themselves to a supranatural being and clung to their selfish desire for salvation.

The socialist ideal of a just society is something like the Kingdom of Heaven without God. In socialism, people as they ought to exist in a just society replace God as the goal toward which all human aspirations are directed. Religion (especially Christianity), which Marx called "the opiate of the masses," is *the* ideological competitor, and Christian churches, even more than liberal states, have been generally viewed as the enemy. It is true that some socialists, such as Karl Kautsky, have preferred to emphasize the links between socialism and early Christianity, and there have been Christian socialists who identified the mission of the Church with the socialist agenda. This tendency is sometimes referred to as the "Social Gospel." Much Christian socialist doctrine consists of interpreting the Christian moral tradition—its emphasis on charity and on communal responsibility—in a socialist light. Socialists are particularly common within the Catholic Church despite the condemnations of socialism and liberalism issued by nineteenth and twentieth century popes. Speaking in broad terms, however, socialists and Christians have usually been rivals and often outright enemies.

Outside of Great Britain, socialist parties have been generally secularist and anticlerical. Anticlericalism, which originated in the Renaissance and the Enlightenment, became a potent political force during the French Revolution, when the properties of the Catholic Church were confiscated, the Church itself was nationalized and turned into the cult of the "Supreme Being," and many Catholics, not only nuns and priests, but ordinary people, suffered persecution and death. In attacking the Catholic Church and offering a weak substitute, the revolutionaries were only acting out the ideas of Jean-Jacques Rousseau, who had called for the creation of a civil religion to which all citizens would be forced to subscribe.

For over a century the French Republic remained the extreme case of an anticlerical state, though other states, such as Italy, also confiscated church property, expelled the Jesuits (an influential teaching order), and took over religious schools. After the Russian Revolution, the U.S.S.R. initiated another round of violent persecutions and repressions, though Stalin, during World War II, relaxed some restrictions and sought religious support for his defense of Russia from the Germans.

The Soviet Union's anti-Christian policies were imitated, to one degree or another, by its satellites in Eastern Europe and by the nonaligned Yugoslavia. In the years following World War II, the communist government of Yugoslavia jailed and executed many members of the clergy, partly because of the Marxists' hostility to religion, but also because, in the Balkans, religion is closely related to ethnic identity: Slovenes and Croats are Catholic, Serbs are Orthodox, Kosovo Albanians and "Bosniaks" (Bosnian Muslims) are Muslim. Communist leaders were fully aware that the greatest obstacle to creating a unified Yugoslavia was ethnic and religious nationalism.

Postwar Yugoslavia, though somewhat milder than other communist regimes, confiscated much of the property of the Serbian Orthodox and Roman Catholic churches, infiltrated monasteries and seminaries, and tried to control the hierarchy through its agents. This caused a split in the Serbian Orthodox Church outside Yugoslavia. Some remained loyal to the Serbian Orthodox patriarch (the head of the church), while others condemned the hierarchy as collaborators with an atheist regime. If the goal was to eliminate Christian traditions and ethnic tensions, Yugoslavia's wars against religion were a total failure, and within ten years of Tito's death, every republic witnessed an upsurge in religious devotion and ethnic patriotism.

Revolutionary Mexico also confiscated church properties and attacked the religion of the overwhelming majority of Mexicans. The attack on the Catholic Church reached its peak in the presidency of Plutarco Calles, who initiated a tough crackdown in 1926 and forbade the celebration of mass. The result was a rebellion of Christian peasants whose slogan was "Viva Cristo Rey" (Long live Christ the king). These rebels, known as Cristeros, maintained an open armed struggle for three years. In the war that suppressed them, they lost 70,000 lives.

Under international pressure, President Calles ended the war, but the persecution of the Church continued well into the 1930s. In some Mexican states, priests were hounded down and murdered, a persecution that inspired Graham Greene's novel, *The Power and the Glory*. President Lázaro Cárdenas (1934–1940) took the first steps to heal the breach between the national government and the religion of the people, but the Catholic Church is still forced to operate under government restrictions that would be unthinkable in most European states.

Socialists and leftists in Western Europe and the United States have been more circumspect, and while it has often proved difficult for a practicing French Catholic to advance very high in a political or military career, church and state in France still collaborate in a variety of ways. Religious schools, for example, receive state subsidies. In the United States, the situation more complex. Most Americans would say that

Lázaro Cárdenas

Lázaro Cárdenas was one of the most significant and revered presidents in the history of Mexico. Born in 1899 to a middle-class family, he worked a variety of jobs, after his father's death, to support his mother and siblings. The young Cárdenas entered politics as a supporter of Plutarco Calles, who made him governor of his native state (Michoacán) in 1928. His honest and effective administration quickly made him popular. Mexico has a one-term limit, but President Calles remained effectively in power by arranging the election of a series of supporters. Cárdenas refused to play the game and exiled the corrupt Calles and many of his top officials. Cárdenas is respected to this day, not only for his honesty but for his independence. As a democratic socialist, he nationalized foreign oil interests and redistributed millions of acres to the peasants, but as a patriotic pragmatist, he worked out the de facto reconciliation with the Catholic Church. A less attractive part of his legacy is the weakened state of property rights, which he made dependent on the government and the ruling party, and the power he amassed for the party, the Institutional Revolutionary Party (PRI).

theirs is a religious, even a Judeo-Christian country, but government policies have minimized church-state collaboration more effectively in the United States than in France. This requires some explanation.

In the United States, where over 90 percent of Americans profess some religious faith (predominantly Christian), the principle of "separation of church and state" has been invoked to exclude religion from schools and public life. This doctrine of separation—or "wall of separation"—owes something to a letter Thomas Jefferson wrote to a group of Connecticut Baptists, is not, as is often stated, written into the Constitution, though it has been defended by the Supreme Court. In fact, the First Amendment to the Constitution explicitly forbids Congress (that is, the federal government) from interfering in the practice or establishment of religion. The Fourteenth Amendment, which was drafted to grant political and legal rights to former slaves, has also been used to justify the exclusion of religion from public places, but no legal scholar has been sufficiently adroit to show that the framers of either the First or the Fourteenth Amendment had the slightest intention of interfering in the practice of religion. What, then, has happened?

One partial explanation is that liberal and left-liberal members of the American political class (including judges) have absorbed the anti-clerical attitude of most socialist and leftist movements, but, as usually happens in Britain and the United States, they prefer to work out a compromise with the religion of the majority rather than engage in open conflict. The solution—permit freedom of religion everywhere except in public places paid for by the taxes of the religious majority—pleases few people entirely but prevents (for the most part) serious hostilities from breaking out. As in the case of abortion, church and state are more controversial in the United States than in Europe, where laws were made not by judges but by democratically elected legislatures.

THE BROTHERHOOD OF MAN

Most socialists have preached a secular version of the Christian "brotherhood of man." On this principle they are opposed to national-ism, wars, colonialism, and the exploitation of underdeveloped countries. Socialist internationalism has been expressed in many different ways. In World War I many socialists in Europe and the United States were pacifists. In England, George Bernard Shaw compared the combatants to pirate ships, though he later conceded that it made a difference which pirate ship you happened to be on. In

Italy, the Socialist Party opposed Italy's entrance into the same war. One of the party leaders, Benito Mussolini, broke with the socialists and endorsed the war. That was the beginning of the Fascist Party, which combined nationalist politics with socialist economics.

Marxist socialism was internationalist from the beginning. Marx and Engels viewed the nation-state (along with the family and private property) as an institution that had been created by patriarchal men solely for the purpose of oppressing women and the poor. In the *Communist Manifesto*, they wrote the blueprint, not merely for communist revolutions, but for an international order that would ultimately replace communist nation-states: "The workers have no country. We cannot take from them what they have not got." The first goal was for the workers to take over nation-states, but ultimately those states, responsible for so many wars and so much antagonism, would be eliminated. The first steps in this direction, they said, had already been taken by liberal governments that promoted global commerce, and this development would be accelerated when the proletariat took power.

Marx and Engels, who should be included among the founders of internationalism, foresaw a time when economic justice would be accomplished not only between the rich and poor of one nation but between rich and poor nations. In the *Communist Manifesto* they confidently predicted:

> In proportion as the exploitation of one individual by another will be put an end to, the exploitation of one nation by another will also be put an end to. In proportion as the antagonism between classes within the nation vanishes, the hostility of one nation to another will come to an end.

Socialists and communists have quite rightly condemned the antagonisms, bigotry, and conflicts produced by national chauvinism. Marxist theory, however, has done little to alleviate ethnic and national hostilities, and Marx and Engels were not without their own ethnic prejudices. They viewed certain ethnic groups, such as Highland Scots, Africans, and Jews as obstacles to progress that had to be suppressed or eliminated. Marx, who supported the North in the U.S. Civil War (known then as the War Between the States) but had initially opposed the emancipation of American slaves, frequently described his son-in-law and disciple, Paul Lafargue, who was purportedly one-eighth African, as "the gorilla."

Though Marx (the grandson of a rabbi) was himself ethnically Jewish, and Jews were prominent in the leadership of most socialist parties, Marx and Engels were openly anti-Semitic in their writings, and the Soviet Union under Stalin eliminated most of the Jewish leaders of the party during the Purge trials. Most were either executed or died in the Gulag. Marx's repellant bigotry has been matched by the record of communist states in persecuting or suppressing ethnic groups. Soviet Russia colonized Ukraine and Lithuania and perse-cuted both Jews and Christians; Communist China subjugated Mongols, Tibetans, and Muslim peoples and set up its own "independent" Catholic Church. Communist states have engaged in aggressive wars even with other communist states (e.g., between Vietnam and Cambodia). And, whatever else can be said of socialist Yugoslavia, it did little to resolve the ethnic tensions that led to its demise.

Socialists and communists in Africa and Latin America are hardly models of ethnic tolerance. Fidel Castro enhanced his international reputation by exporting black Cubans to fight in African wars, and no Mexican government has made much progress in improving the lot of indigenous Mexicans (about half the population). Their living conditions in southern Mexico are so poor that Native Americans have risen up repeatedly. In Chiapas State the Zapatista uprising of the 1990s was put down with considerable force, and the quasisocialist Mexican government has been repeatedly accused of employing paramilitary forces to intimidate the Zapatistas.

The more stable socialist governments of Europe have a better record of promoting human brotherhood. At the beginning of World War II, the British Labour Party had declared, as one of its peace aims, "a new world order . . . securely founded on socialism and democracy." For the postwar party, the glaring problem to be addressed was Britain's colonial empire, which the socialists had repeatedly denounced. The Atlee government rapidly took steps toward dismantling the British Empire, granting independence to India, Pakistan, and what was then known as Transjordan. The withdrawal from India and Pakistan, arranged by Lord Mountbatten, was done in reckless haste, with little concern for the interests of the Muslims. The result was a fierce national war between India and Pakistan and a religious war between Hindus and Muslims. The repercussions are still felt today. Good intentions are rarely sufficient to guarantee peace and justice in a postcolonial world.

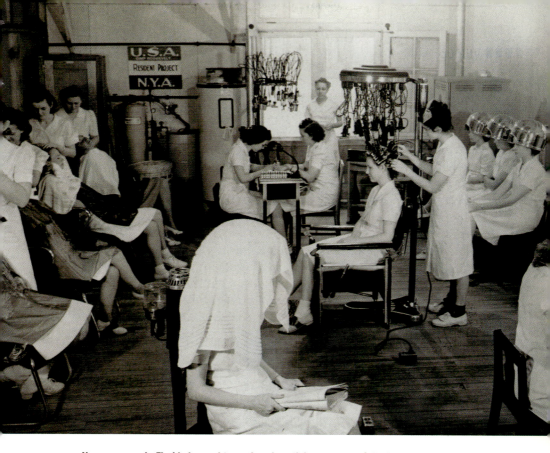

Young women in Florida learned to work as beauticians as part of the National Youth Administration set up in the 1930s. During the Great Depression, President Franklin D. Roosevelt's administration set up many far-reaching employment programs.

As Britain and France abandoned their empires, the United States and the U.S.S.R. were building theirs. The Soviet Union's domination of Eastern Europe caused many European leftists to denounce Stalin, while the United States, in taking up the burden of defending Vietnam from the French, became the symbol (to the European Left) of aggressive nationalism. Since U.S. power rested ultimately on "the bomb," leftists were opposed to nuclear weapons, and those who were soft on the Soviet Union also favored unilateral disarmament, a position that seriously damaged Britain's Labour Party. In the 1960s the reputation of the United States was at an all-time low in Europe and among leftists, and, although anti-American passions cooled, they broke out again during the Iraq War (2003–). It was not so much the "American way of life," much less the American people that aroused hatred, but the perception that America was the last state to harbor nationalist and imperialist ambitions.

The most radical version of the leftist critique of the West's relations with the Third World uses terms such as exploitation and alienation. Frantz Fanon, in two influential books (*Black Skin, White Mask* and *The Wretched of the Earth*), argued that European colonizers had robbed their Third World victims of language and identity. Thus to be a nonwhite in a white world led to a sense of psychological alienation. "Whiteness," for Fanon, was a basically negative category that relegated the nonwhite to nonexistence. The Palestinian historian, Edward Said, developed a similar line of reasoning in books exploring relations between the European West and the Islamic East.

Fanon grew progressively more radical, and in *The Wretched of the Earth*, he called for little less than the extermination of European civilization by violent revolution. His arguments and rhetoric have been repeated endlessly by radicals and would-be revolutionaries of the 1960s and later by the proponents of multiculturalism who opposed the teaching of Western Civilization courses. As popular as he was to become after his death in 1961, Fanon was hardly an original thinker. Most of his case against Western civilization had already been made by French communists and surrealists of the 1920s and 1930s, while his treatment of alienation had been anticipated by neo-Marxists such as the Hungarian Georgy Lukacs and the leaders of the Frankfurt School.

The language of colonial exploitation has been taken up by many dissident movements, most of them leftist or socialist like the Irish Republican Army, the Parti Québecquois in Canada, Basque separatists in Spain, and—paradoxically—by white nationalists and the "Men's Movement" in the United States. In Mexico, the official ideology of the regime includes the story of the wicked *conquistadores*, who overthrew brilliant indigenous civilizations and exploited their conquered subjects until the oppressed natives freed themselves first from Spain and then, in the Mexican Revolution, from the Spanish rancheros who had continued to exploit the peasants. A far more radical version of this account is given by Chicano studies professors in the United States, whose influence on the Mexican-American community has been frequently exaggerated by opponents of immigration.

ECONOMIC GLOBALISM

A logical conclusion, from the socialist perspective on the international order, is that some of the resources of the developed world are owed to

Frankfurt School

The Frankfurt School, which began in 1923 as The Institute for Social Research at Frankfurt University (Germany), was an influential tradition of Marxist social theory. In its early days, the Institute was home to Marxist theorists Max Horkheimer (who became director in 1930), Theodor Adorno, Walter Benjamin, Jürgen Habermas, and Herbert Marcuse. Since neither Jews nor Marxists were welcome in Nazi Germany, many members fled to New York in 1933 and affiliated themselves with The New School for Social Research at Columbia University. Although Horkheimer and Adorno returned to Frankfurt in 1953, their students were located in important universities in Europe and the United States.. The Frankfurt School approach, often known as "Critical Theory," takes Marx's early works as a starting point and subjects social and cultural institutions to a skeptical analysis that regards them as the ideological instruments by which a ruling class holds power. If, for example, a ruling class emphasizes obedience to authority, it will require strong authoritarian fathers and teachers, who will teach obedience and respect for authority to the youth. Herbert Marcuse, who taught at Harvard, Brandeis, and the University of California-San Diego, exerted a strong influence on 1960s radicals and became known as the "Father of the New Left."

Combining Marx and the psychoanalytical approach to sex, Marcuse argued (in his book *One Dimensional Man* and in a famous essay, "Repressive Tolerance") that people were not really free, but, dominated by what he called "false values," they were induced to work far more than necessity dictated. As a part of his project of liberation, he advocated something like "sex, drugs, and rock and roll." Until his death in 1979, Marcuse was a favorite target of academic conservatives.

developing countries. Global philanthropy is the principle of the national welfare state applied internationally. Because of injustices committed by previous generations of Europeans, developed nations today should promote the economic and social progress of developing countries.

There are dozens of international manifestos and charters that call for a just (that is, redistributive) global economy. The United Nations' 1974 "Declaration of the Establishment of a New International Order," for example, proclaims a "united determination . . . to correct inequalities and redress existing injustices . . . to eliminate the widening gap between the developed and developing countries," and the "Charter of Economic Rights and Duties of States" recognizes the rights of states "to nationalize, expropriate or transfer ownership of foreign property."

International development has outgrown socialist ideology: it is an issue where socialism and liberal capitalism converge. Free-market liberals look on national boundaries, which impede the flow of goods and labor, with a skepticism almost equal to that of Marxists. Friedrich Hayek, one of socialism's most stringent critics, agrees with socialists (against conservatives and nationalists) that national competition is a danger to peace:

> It is neither necessary nor desirable that national
> boundaries should mark sharp differences in standards of
> living, that membership of a national group should entitle
> [it]to a share of the cake altogether different from that in
> which members of other groups share.

In a normal world, individuals trade with other individuals around the globe, but "when international economic relations . . . become increasingly relations between whole nations organized as trading bodies, they inevitably become the source of friction and envy between whole nations." Global free trade, in other words, eliminates conflicts between nations because it eliminates the economic significance of the nations themselves. Liberals and libertarians agree with socialists on the desirability of an international economic order that eliminates national distinctions, though socialists would put more emphasis on the duty of the West to elevate the prosperity of poor nations.

For socialists the goal is improving the condition of the poor, but capitalists and neoliberals have contributed the principle that this can only be done when there is integration into world markets. This is the argument used by the Brandt Commission (chaired by the German socialist leader Willy Brandt) and other proponents of international aid. The European left generally supports both aid to the Third World and global economic integration. One analyst of French socialism sums up the sentiment in his country: "No political force can any longer aspire to govern on the basis of even a partial isolation of France from the global economy."

The exceptions in France are the leaders of the National Front (right-wing nationalists) and groups on the left and right that oppose European integration. In Britain, opponents include the small British National Party and a minority of Conservatives (so-called "Euroskeptics"), and in America a left/right convergence that includes Ralph Nader and Patrick J. Buchanan. Mainstream parties, however, parties "that aspire to govern," all speak the language of free trade and global integration, spiced with an insistence upon humanitarian assistance.

There is more than a hint of ethnocentrism in the argument for global integration. It is based on the assumption that people in the developed West lead happier lives than the peoples of poor countries. There is absolutely no evidence that this is so, as economist Lord Peter Bauer has pointed out, and there is no reason to believe that people in Third World countries actually desire the modernization that Western countries are so eager to provide. Some leftist socialists agree, and the antiglobalist movement is dominated by the far left, as is evident from the people who turn out for the hostile demonstrations that greet international economic conferences.

This is not really a paradox. Some Western socialists have grown tired of an ideology that reduces human life to so many years of schooling, so many square feet of housing space, so many hours of work a day, and so many weeks of paid vacation time. More "primitive" cultures seem to offer a more communitarian, more spiritual, more natural alternative, which should be preserved from the steamroller of progress and modernization. Marx would no doubt have been appalled, but socialist dissatisfaction with materialism and consumerism manifests itself in many ways, but particularly in the attraction of more "spiritual" political movements like environmentalism.

ENVIRONMENTALISM

"Why are environmentalist parties like a tomato?" asks an Italian joke of the 1990s. Answer: "Because they start out green but they turn red before your very eyes." The germ of truth in this joke is that Green parties are generally made up of socialists and leftists who added environmentalism to their agenda without giving up their commitment to Marxism. Green parties in Europe (especially in Germany) also advocate feminist and pacifist policies as well as nationalization of major industries. In Germany they support stridently anti-American policies, evidenced by the fact that "they fought more against nuclear missiles than against nuclear reactors."

Most Western European countries had Green parties by the middle of the 1980s. Though none of these parties ever came close to winning an election or even winning 10 percent of the total vote in an election, they had surprising influence. Some tried to work in coalition with socialist parties, as in Germany where collaboration with the socialist party split the Greens, though it put Green Party leader Joschka Fischer (a former supporter of the revolutionary left) into influential cabinet posts. Elsewhere, Green parties have served more as pressure groups that forced major parties across the political spectrum to pay more attention to environmental issues. In the United States, the Green Party was the focal point of antiglobal, anti-free-trade, anti-imperial, and antiwar protests in which they were joined by anti-war libertarians and conservatives.

For many Greens, one popular cutting-edge issue has been nuclear power. In a period of rising oil prices, traditional leftist parties were reluctant to abandon nuclear power but the energy crisis cut both ways. While some voters tended to conclude that oil shortages only increased the attractiveness of nuclear energy, others favored sources of energy (such as solar and wind power) that proponents claimed were less damaging to the environment.

As socialists adopted the cultural and political agenda of the more radical left, they risked losing support from the industrial workers who had been their core constituency. In many countries, not just Britain and the United States, blue-collar workers are often moral and social conservatives. While they support welfare-state policies, many are opposed to abortion and the more radical programs of minority rights. Nonetheless, alienation from the workers may not matter a great deal in the long run. In developed countries, industrial workers, many of whom have long since joined the middle class, are a dwindling minority in economic systems increasingly based on information technology. It is very possible that the next generation of socialists will be far more green than red.

Green Parties

Green Party members all over the world, including those shown here in Moscow, protest environmental pollution.

Green parties and movements are generally dedicated to environment-alism. The Four Pillars of official Green parties are Ecology, Justice, Democracy, and Peace. This means that, on principle, they oppose war and favor vigorous laws protecting the environment, special protection for the poor and, and for ethnic, religious, and sexual minorities, decentralized political decisionmaking. The first Green party (The United Tasmania Group) was formed in Tasmania in 1972, and it was quickly followed by the establishment of similar parties in Canada, the UK, and Europe. A Charter of the Global Greens was adopted at an international meeting in Canberra, Australia, in 2001. There are now Green parties all over the world. For a list and a copy of the charter, see http://www.greens.org.

Environmentalism and same-sex marriage seem a far cry from the economic revolution demanded by the *Communist Manifesto*, but socialism can be viewed as something more than a nineteenth and twentieth century political movement. It is also one phase in a revolutionary tradition that goes back at least as far as the Renaissance. As years and decades go by, the target of the revolution changes its name and even its identity. Once upon a time the enemies were feudalism, the Catholic Church, and the "Dark Ages." Later on the hostility was first directed against kings, then capitalists, then domineering Caucasian males. Underlying all these evolutions and transformations, however, is a basic formula: In each case there is a ruthless ruling class that exploits an endless series of victims—laymen, peasants, workers, the environment. Since "man's inhumanity to man" has been part of the human condition as it is known throughout history, the socialist revolution will never run out of enemies.

6

Achievements and Criticism ■ ■ ■

MODERN SOCIALISM BEGAN AS A THEORY of justice and as a dream of rebuilding a social and economic order that had been shattered by the French Revolution and its aftershocks. In the hands of Marx and his later disciples, socialism became a complete political ideology that combined theories of history (class conflict) and economics (the labor theory of value), and justice (empowerment of the proletariat). In the roughly 150 years that followed the publication of the *Communist Manifesto* (1847), socialist models have been implemented by revolutionary communists and social democrats and analyzed and attacked by non-socialist political theorists. It *should* be possible to draw up a balance sheet of successes and failures. Unfortunately neither socialists nor their enemies seem very interested in offering a balanced analysis.

For socialists, every failure or atrocity is the result of the wrong men (Stalin, Mao Zedong, Pol Pot) getting into power, global economic crisis (depression, inflation, oil prices), or not really a failure at all, only a success that has been misrepresented by critics (e.g., the Yugoslav "miracle," high literacy rates in Cuba and Nicaragua). For critics of socialism, the balance sheet is dripping in the red ink of debts and slow growth as well as the red blood of the victims of communist repression, while lengthened lifespans and improved health care are ignored. Under these circumstances an author might be suspected of hypocrisy if he claimed to be completely impartial. Perhaps the best that can be done is to give an objective evaluation of socialist aims and, in assessing results, to present arguments from both sides.

SOCIALISM: SCIENCE OR IDEOLOGY

Socialist ideas, long before any were proposed or enacted by political parties, have been subjected to searching criticisms. Aristotle argued against most of the key points of Plato's *Republic* and *Laws*. To oppose the equality of Plato's Guardians, Aristotle distinguished between two kinds of equality: arithmetical equality, which gives equal shares and privileges to everyone, and proportional equality, which assigns greater rewards (of wealth, power, etc.) to those who contribute the most, by defending and governing the country and by supporting it with their wealth. This was part of Aristotle's general theory that a mixed constitution, that is, one that combined the strengths of monarchy, aristocracy, and democracy, was the best system.

As critical as he was of egalitarian democracy, Aristotle was equally suspicious of any proposal to invest virtuous philosophers or technocrats with absolute power. His most fundamental criticism was against what might be called Plato's *angelism,* that is, his refusal to accept humankind as it is and his habit of treating people as if they were angels or demigods, capable of infinite improvement. While Plato had imagined that a society could be ruled by a class of Guardians who shared all property and wealth, Aristotle insisted that both family life and property are natural to man and constitute part of the good life. After nearly 2,400 years, Aristotle remains the most profound critic of socialist theory.

Even in principle, though Marx would have denied it, socialism requires a powerful government directed by unselfish experts. The French utopian Count Saint-Simon called for a draconian system to punish resistance to his perfect society, and his disciples went still further in rejecting the liberal values of freedom and democracy. Auguste Comte's positivist social structures, which had to be designed and managed by objective social engineers, were a step further in the direction of the total state, a concept that was perfected and put into operation by Lenin. Built into socialist theory, from Plato to the present, is the usually unspoken assumption that most people are too blinded by selfishness to know what they really need. Their economic choices and social decisions, therefore, must be controlled by a set of guardians or party leaders, who are only interested in helping other people.

Consider the simple example of public education in the United States. Today we take state-controlled education for granted, but there was a time (roughly until the U.S. Civil War) when schooling was in the hands of families, churches, and small communities. In the nineteenth century, advocates of public education declared that farm families and immigrant parents were so narrow-minded that they would have put their children to work rather than send them to school. Some of this thinking was influenced by the autocratic Prussian state, but it was also encouraged by German socialist refugees from the Revolution of 1848. Rural and small-town school districts, supported solely by local taxes, were said to be too stingy and unprogressive to maintain high standards. Therefore, according to progressive theory, the many small local school systems had to be consolidated into giant districts, subjected to tight state regulation, and filled with students who, if they failed to attend, were subject to truancy and delinquency laws.

There was little evidence to back up the claims made for progressive educational programs. Even in the first generation of school consolidation, the new schools cost far more but failed to improve educational standards. In fact, some superior students made more rapid progress in rural one-room schoolhouses than in well-funded consolidated schools in big cities. Later, as more and more school district income was redistributed from rich to poor districts, good results were just as hard to find. This did not deter the experts, who were convinced that they knew better than parents what was best for the children. The whole public school debate, which raged from the 1840s to the 1950s, was predicated on a basic socialist assumption: Wise technocrats had to make decisions for selfish and unenlightened parents.

American parents may well have been as uneducated, selfish, and unenlightened as they were portrayed by the experts, but, as James Buchanan (Nobel laureate in economics) and Gordon Tulloch have shown, educators, bureaucrats, and politicians are no more immune to selfish temptations than the rest of us are. According to this school of thought, known as Public Choice Theory, the managers of state agencies will always act in such a way as to increase the power and wealth of their agency (and thus of themselves). This is almost always at the expense of taxpaying citizens who do not work for the government. A more popular, but equally accurate critique of bureaucracy was provided by Northcote Parkinson, who authored Parkinson's Law, which states "work expands so as to fill the time

Milovan Djilas was a leading communist guerrilla in Yugoslavia during World War II. In the postwar era, he became a leading socialist intellectual. A sharp critic of Communism, he was jailed several times by the communist government he had once served.

available for its completion." Parkinson's Law is often misunderstood as a bit of sly humor, but, in fact, Parkinson was a shrewd economic thinker who provided a devastating analysis of how bureaucrats expand the size of their office without accomplishing more work.

In education, this meant bigger schools, more and more administrators, ever-increasing budgets that were matched all over the United States by declining test scores. While nationwide budgets rose by a rate of 500 percent (adjusted for inflation) in the four decades after World War II, student performance declined. One important factor was the power of administrators and union officials, who campaigned for increases in staff size, salaries, and benefits, but tended to neglect the fundamentals: good teachers and effective textbooks. American education is a simple example of a situation that can be analyzed by Public Choice Theory, but an analysis of welfare, environmental, and regulatory agencies yields the same results. People are people, whether we call them guardians, commissars, teachers, social workers, or Princes of the Church. During the Russian Revolution, W. H. Mallock, after studying the power-seeking behavior of socialist leaders, had predicted that socialism would lead to bureaucratic tyranny.

A similar criticism of the socialist elite was made by Milovan

Milovan Djilas

Milovan Djilas was one of the most controversial socialist leaders of the twentieth century. Born in a village of Montenegro in 1911, Djilas joined the Communist Party in 1932 when he was a university student. He was one of the leaders of the communist Partisan movement during World War II and a close associate of Josip Broz, who took the party name of Tito. Backed by the U.S.S.R. and eventually by the allies, the communist Partisans fought both the Germans and Yugoslavs loyal to the government in exile. Although an intellectual, Djilas was long resented for his ferocity and cruelty toward his enemies. In 1944 Djilas was sent by Tito to Moscow to conduct negotiations with Stalin. After the war, he was one of the two or three most influential members of Tito's government, and he was sent again in 1948 to discuss Yugoslav complaints against Stalin's attempt to control postwar Yugoslavia. His criticisms of the harsh regime imposed by Tito and of the corruption of party members led to his imprisonment on several occasions. Although he remained a socialist, he also supported democracy and freedom of speech. He is best remembered for a series of important books: *The New Class*, *Conversations with Stalin*, which subjected communism to a serious and scathing critique, and books about his own life and the history of the tiny Serbian land of Montenegro: *Land Without Justice*, *Wartime*, and *Njegos*. By his courageous and outspoken criticisms, Djilas won the respect of the world, though not the affection of non-communists in Yugoslavia. Before he died in 1991, the elderly atheist requested an Orthodox Christian funeral, but after the service, his grave was desecrated by those who remembered his wartime atrocities in Montenegro.

Djilas, one of the leaders of the Yugoslav Communist Party. Djilas had personal knowledge of the graft and corruption that was rampant among his colleagues. In *The New Class*, he portrayed the socialist elite as no better than a more powerful substitute for the capitalist ruling class. Analyzing the policies of nationalization and collectivization, he remarked that communists eliminate all forms of property but their own, that is, under socialism, party officials monopolize control (and thus the benefits) of great property and wealth. Confirming the accuracy of his observations, the Yugoslav government sentenced Djilas to several prison terms.

Built into the theory of socialism is a basic contradiction. Following Rousseau, socialists believe that people are basically good, but they have been exploited and subjugated by those who control the institutions of the church, the state, and the market. But if power corrupts, then how can we expect a new ruling class to be exempt from the temptation to subjugate and exploit? It is an old insight, made famous by the Roman poet Juvenal. If we empower guardians to keep watch over us, *Quis custodiet ipsos custodes?* ("Who will guard the guardians themselves?")

A second charge, leveled against Marxist socialism in particular, is that it pretends to be science or philosophy but is neither. It cannot be a true philosophy, which is a search for truth, because Marxism aims at gaining and exercising power. Truth, as many Marxists have proclaimed, is whatever serves the needs of the proletarian revolution. But Marx's "scientific socialism" is not science either. Few of Marx's theoretical formulations can be tested, and those that can be tested—his economic predictions of imminent revolution, for example—have not proved to be accurate.

As Mallock pointed out in *A Critical Examination of Socialism* (1908), most of Marx's own followers had quietly abandoned much of his economic theory—including his faith that socialism could arrive spontaneously—before the end of the nineteenth century. Of the key socialist articles of faith—government ownership of the means of production, equalized wages, the dictatorship of the proletariat—few are now accepted even by radical socialists. But this objection is not necessarily fatal. Some later Marxists, for example Georgy Lukacs (but also Frankfurt School theorists), have insisted that even if Marx were proved wrong on every specific point, it would not matter, because Marxism is essentially a method, a way of looking at human societies as class conflicts.

If Marxist theory is neither science nor philosophy, then what is it? Marx would have described such a system of thought as an ideology, an orderly presentation of theories that are intended to produce and justify a certain kind of regime. Marx applied such an analysis to liberal and democratic theories, whose purpose, so he believed, was to justify capitalist exploitation. Marxism, similarly, has been used to justify the power of socialist and left-liberal establishments.

Despite the lack of scientific rigor, Marxism as a revolutionary ideal is still capable of firing the imagination. What is more, Marx had considerable originality as a social critic and philosopher of history. Though few non-Marxists have accepted his view that history is reducible to a series of inevitable class conflicts over material resources and means of production, Marx was among the few people of his age to have realized that nineteenth century capitalism was not a traditional economic system but part of a revolution that had transformed the world. Critical Marxist theory remains a valuable tool of analysis that can be employed by conservatives as much as by leftists.

Marx also saw what classical liberals refused to see, namely, that industrial capitalism had undermined all the security enjoyed by poor people in traditional societies. Uprooted from agricultural villages and put to work in mines and factories with their wives and children, proletarian workers lacked the safety net of extended families and closely knit circles of friends. Workers had no culture, traditions, or religion to fall back on, and, taught the hard lessons of dog-eat-dog economics by capitalist employers, workers became eager to claim their share of the wealth.

Critics of socialism point out the obvious fact that Marx was wrong in predicting the course of "the revolution." Revolutions were not, by and large, fought and won by the industrial proletariat of economically developed nations. In fact, revolutions only succeeded in underdeveloped countries, such as Russia, China, Vietnam, Cambodia, and Cuba. Britain, France, and the United States (like most developed countries) avoided revolution. Yes, the socialists answered, but they only avoided revolution by adopting socialist measures such as social security and health insurance programs, unemployment and disability compensation, public housing, and free or subsidized education from early childhood through professional postgraduate degrees. In the nineteenth and early twentieth centuries, more than one conservative (e.g., Sir Walter Scott, George Fitzhugh, G. K. Chesterton) argued that liberal societies, based on freedom and equality, would always

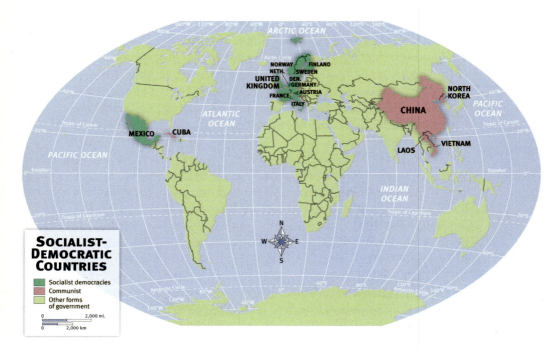

Socialist-Democratic Countries

subject the weak and incompetent to subjugation by the strong and capable. The inevitable result, they predicted, would be some form of socialism. In the 1940s, Joseph Schumpeter sharply analyzed the creative destruction wrought by capitalist societies that undermined their own foundations and prepared the ground for socialism.

EFFICIENCY OR SOCIAL JUSTICE?

Until the early twentieth century, critiques of socialism remained, of necessity, at the theoretical level, but once socialist parties began implementing their programs, a series of distinguished economists and political thinkers mounted a sustained attack that has proved to be more effective than socialists had anticipated. There are several types of criticisms of socialism. The most fundamental, though least frequent, line of attack is against the core principles of socialism. Redistribution of wealth can be regarded as fundamentally unjust because it deprives human beings of their right to own property and the need to exercise charity. A more common argument is that the ever-increasing size and scope of government in socialist and communist states interfere far too much in private life and suppress individual liberty.

Perhaps the most frequent objection is the argument of inefficiency: socialist schemes simply do not work the way they are supposed to or end up costing far too much money. Such criticisms have been forcefully made by the leaders of the so-called Austrian School; Friedrich Hayek, winner of the Nobel Prize in economics; his mentor Ludwig von Mises; and by Milton Friedman (another Nobel laureate), who focused much of his attack on Keynesian economics.

Hayek's *The Road to Serfdom* attacked socialist centralized planning even before such policies had been widely implemented outside the U.S.S.R. For Hayek, the central problem was knowledge. The fluctuation of prices in free markets is a constant source of key data that enable business managers to make correct decisions or at least decisions that are in tune with competitors, suppliers, and customers. An uncentralized and largely unregulated system of pricing is the only one that can work, says Hayek, "because nobody can consciously balance all the considerations bearing on the decisions of so many individuals, the coordination can clearly be effected not by 'conscious control'". . . . To the socialist argument that, while free markets might have worked in primitive times, modern complex economies require scientific planning, Hayek responds that the price system becomes more necessary as division of labor and specialization increase, precisely because of the greater need for a wide variety of complex information from many sources. The price system, under competition, he wrote, "enables entrepreneurs, by watching the movement of comparatively few prices, as an engineer watches the hands of a few dials, to adjust their activities to those of their fellows."

The most telling criticism against communism was the record of communist states: the tens of millions executed and starved to death, the massive concentration camps whose harsh conditions have been documented by Alexander Solzhenitsyn. The criticism is certainly just, insofar as the U.S.S.R., China, Cambodia, and Vietnam are concerned, but of the "softer" socialist states that were independent, only Yugoslavia has much of a record of violent repression, and even Yugoslavia, after a fairly brief period of imitating the U.S.S.R., became a calm and *comparatively* free society in an Eastern Europe dominated by totalitarian repression. It is not clear that a socialist Poland or Czechoslovakia would have been as harsh as the Soviet-controlled

Friedrich Hayek

Born in Vienna in 1899, Friedrich Hayek received degrees in law and political science from the University of Vienna, but he also studied economics under leaders of the Austrian School. In 1931 he went to London to teach at the London School of Economics and became a British subject in 1938. In 1950 he went to the University of Chicago, though his ties to the Austrian School prevented him from teaching in the economics department. Hayek was among the outstanding liberal-libertarian critics of socialism in the twentieth century. Much of his critique was directed against Keynesian planning and what Hayek regarded as the delusion that an economy could be planned and managed. The system of wages and prices that developed in a free market could not be planned, he argued, but represented a tendency toward "spontaneous order." Hayek's ideas, condemned initially, exercised a direct influence on politicians like Margaret Thatcher and a more general indirect influence on classical liberal and conservative movements in Britain and the United States.

Hayek broadened his critique of planning to include "scientism," that is, the belief that science could be used to reconstruct human society. Hayek, later in life, came to understand that economic and political freedom could not be treated as absolutes but had to be justified by moral and cultural principles. Not long before his death in 1992, his book *The Fatal Conceit* eloquently took up and developed the philosophical ideas on which his work was based. To illustrate the split brain of economic and political thought, Hayek shared the 1974 Nobel Prize in Economics with the Keynesian socialist Gunnar Myrdal.

puppets of the Warsaw Pact (the alliance of the U.S.S.R. and its subject nations). On the other hand, democratic-socialist states have not escaped the charge of being run by meddlesome do-gooders whose interventions in the free market and in private life have produced dullness, sterility, and dependency.

Mallock predicted, and Hayek and Mises criticized, the economic stagnation of socialism, but they were not lone voices. George Orwell, in his novel *1984*, portrayed a bleak world of state-controlled economic systems in which plodding obedient subjects were brainwashed by the state-controlled media. Orwell had been a leftist and never became a classical liberal, much less a conservative, but he was only one of many former communists and lapsed leftists who repudiated, as one book title put it, *The God That Failed*.

A THIRD WAY

The "total state" is a nightmare to most people, but even milder forms of socialism can seem stultifying and repressive. When film director Ingmar Bergman (hardly a political conservative or classical liberal) went into voluntary exile from Sweden, he denounced the constant meddling of petty bureaucrats who made creative life difficult. Hayek warned that the socialist policies pursued in Great Britain were paving "the road to serfdom," but decades earlier, Hilaire Belloc, a deeper historical thinker than either Hayek or Orwell, used as his title *The Servile State*. Belloc knew that under medieval serfdom, which had been a step away from slavery and toward liberty, serfs had had greater security, but the collectivist policies called for by socialists would *continue* to reduce entire populations (other than a property-owning elite) to moral and spiritual slavery.

Belloc's main target was not, in fact, socialism but state-supported capitalism, which had concentrated the ownership of property and wealth in an ever-decreasing number of hands and was steadily expro-priating the poorer classes. He was astute enough to realize that his own solution—to preserve traditional civilization by redistributing property—called for heroic measures bound to be unpopular, while socialism only asked for a fairly easy transformation of capitalism into a servile collectivist state. The wealthy and powerful would remain wealthy and powerful by working for the government, while the progress toward the servile state would continue without interruption.

Belloc and his friend G. K. Chesterton did not regard themselves as conservatives but as "distributists," since they called for a radical redistribution of property. Their argument was paralleled in the United States by the Southern Agrarians, who contributed to the volume *I'll Take My Stand* (1930) and joined forces with Belloc in another volume of essays, *Who Owns America?* Opposing industrial capitalism as much as they opposed communism, agrarians and distributists preferred a society made up of small farmers and shopkeepers, where local and regional cultural traditions were preserved and culture was something more than a product sent out to radio stations and movie theaters.

More recent agrarian critics of socialism and industrial society include Richard Weaver, M. E. Bradford, and Wendell Berry. Unlike Hayek and the liberals, distributists and agrarians viewed economic questions in the light of moral, cultural, and spiritual concerns. Some of their views were shared by the Austrian School economist Wilhelm Röpke, who concluded that the liberal antisocialism of Hayek and Mises placed too great an emphasis on profit and too little on the conditions for human happiness. These and other writers are often described as representing a Third Way between socialism and capitalism. Their critique of socialism, because it looks at moral issues, often has more impact than arguments based strictly on the inefficiency of socialism.

Perhaps the worst condemnation of centrally planned economies is not the inefficiency or bureaucracy but the lack of initiative, the drab cultural life, and the sheer ugliness and inhumanity of the housing complexes built for the working poor in cities like Moscow, Bratislava, and Belgrade, or the subsidized housing units in Britain and the United States. For the bureaucratic mind, whether socialist or capitalist, spontaneity and eccentricity are anathema, and human souls must be kept in order like so many concrete blocks in a wall. The convergence of communist, socialist, and capitalist systems has made it difficult to criticize the tendencies of one system without discussing the others. Big government and declining cultural standards are as much a feature of life in the United States as in the Brezhnev era of the Soviet Union or in socialist Sweden. Critiques of socialism, therefore, have often been included in more general critiques of modernity.

The distinction between communism and socialism is largely one of method, since the ultimate goal of the two systems is the same, while the distinction between capitalism and socialism, though real enough in principle, becomes less and less relevant in a system where the state controls and regulates business in favor of the largest corporations, and the corporate managerial class is identical to the managerial class that runs the government. This was the insight of the former Trotskyist James Burnham, in the *Managerial Revolution*, that Stalinism, Hitlerism, and Roosevelt's New Deal were only variations on a theme: Everywhere the managerial class was emerging as the dominant ruling class and remaking societies in its own image.

Another moral argument against big-government political systems including socialism is that they degrade human dignity, producing selfish consumers instead of morally responsible human beings who pursue virtue and excellence. The most influential critique of this kind was made by José Ortega y Gasset in *The Revolt of the Masses*. For Ortega, the very principle of equality, in either its democratic or its socialist form, produced what he called "mass man," the commonplace and unreflective average man who despises high standards and thinks himself qualified to pass judgment on questions he has never studied. Ortega was an aristocratic liberal of the interwar years, but he was far from being the only important twentieth century intellectual to have lamented the death of civilization and the triumph of mediocrity. Even the shortest list would include some of the most profound and influential writers of the twentieth century, such as the American poets T. S. Eliot and Ezra Pound, and the French writers Charles Péguy and Paul Claudel.

Many of the critics of modern mediocrity were Christian conservatives, but not all. After World War II, French existentialists were keen to attack the immorality and lack of authenticity in capitalist societies, though some, like Jean-Paul Sartre, were willfully blind to Stalin's crimes and Soviet imperialism. But Sartre's younger friend, the novelist Albert Camus, was as bitter against the degrading effects of mass society as Ortega, and he did not hesitate to condemn the U.S.S.R. as roundly as he condemned the West. The French Catholic existentialist Gabriel Marcel made a powerful assault on the dehumanizing effects of state bureaucracy, a problem more acute in socialist countries, with their emphasis on central planning, than in capitalist states that still afforded some scope for economic competition.

A QUESTION OF JUSTICE

As Eduard Bernstein and others realized, socialism is in many ways an extension of the liberal agenda, but there are differences. True socialists claim to offer a vision of the good life and a just social system, while liberals claim to be neutral, preferring to allow each individual to pursue his or her own life's interests so long as he does not interfere, through coercive means, with the pursuits of other people. This broad statement needs a little qualification, since few socialists are willing to specify the nature of the good life for any one person. Their ideal has to do with the collective arrangements of society and with the distribution of wealth, goods, and services.

A socialist, when pressed to say why a society should put his vision into action, will say that his ideology is based on history, science, and justice. A classical liberal or libertarian (and many an American "conservative"), when asked the same question, can only repeat that liberty is itself an ultimate good. This may be true, but, like every other ethical principle, it has to be proved. If liberty is going to be treated as a self-evident absolute, then it is a religious and not a political principle.

When liberals of every stripe develop their theories of justice, they count on the fact that their followers share certain prejudices that are widely accepted today. For example, most current forms of liberalism are based on traditional theories of equality or private property or liberty or human rights, but none of these first principles has ever been proved, and each conflicts with the others. In a different place and time, such ideas would seem bizarre. Perhaps the worst mistake made by liberals and socialists is to imagine that all human societies are based on one principle or the other. In fact, neither liberal nor socialist theory is very relevant for understanding an ancient Greek city-state, an Eskimo village, or medieval Europe.

If liberal opponents of socialism usually win the arguments about efficiency, they are defeated rather easily on arguments about justice and morality. In any question involving human value, or justice, or social responsibility, classical liberals and free-market "conservatives" are at a loss. Religious people can invoke divine commandments or the teachings of their church or tradition; socialists and communists, who claim to know what is right for society, can speak of fulfilling iron laws of history; but the liberals and libertarians have nothing to offer in its place except the freedom to choose. Socialists and religious believers, when confronted by the liberal slogan "free to choose," can always ask: Choose what and why? Classical liberals, in the extreme case, reply that asking such a question is evidence of a socialist or fascist mindset, because it is wrong to make judgments about what other people want. This is essentially the view of Mises, who lumps together most political moralists as socialists and reduces society to "the means by which each individual member seeks to attain its own ends"; in other words, to a battlefield of competing egos. Such language may gain a round of applause from doctrinaire libertarians, but in the real world, where people every day have to make important moral decisions within families and communities, such a reply wins few arguments.

THE BALANCE SHEET

Socialism is both a political theory and a type of regime. As a theory, socialism has supplied a powerful critique of liberalism and capitalism, but it has failed to put forward an understanding of society that corresponds to what is known of human nature. Put into practice by socialist and quasi-socialist governments, it has often softened the hard lot of those who have failed to succeed in competitive societies based on the principles of liberty and equality. At its worst, in communist countries and in countries that have adopted scientific socialist planning, socialism has encouraged meddlesome and ambitious politicians and bureaucrats to exercise control over the lives of billions of human beings they neither know nor care about.

Some economic aspects of socialism, however, are probably inevitable in the vast countries and complex economies created by liberals and nationalists over the centuries. Many socialist policies have been generally accepted by non-socialist parties. Winston Churchill supported nationalization, and President George W. Bush advocated something called "compassionate conservatism," which was simply the socialist welfare state as run by the Republican Party. Meanwhile, many socialists and radical leftists have moved on to other issues, such as environmentalism and gender issues. Whether the social revolution will continue its "long march through the institutions" will depend largely on the strength and resilience of those institutions, undermined long ago, as communists and conservatives have argued, by liberal capitalism. For the foreseeable future, though, socialist policies like the graduated income tax, national health insurance, and social security are here to stay. Although Americans do not like to say it, we are all socialists now.

Socialism and Other Governments

SOCIALISM	THEOCRACY	COMMUNISM
Multiple legal political parties;limited electoral freedom	Often only one legal political party	Only one legal political party (Communist Party)
Rule by people through elections, although individual or small group may dominate politics	Limited or no electoral freedom; rule by a single individual or small group	No free elections; rule by a single individual or small group
Opposition and dissent may be limited	Opposition and dissent are limited or forbidden	Opposition and dissent are limited or forbidden
Limited property rights	Limited property rights	No property rights
Government has significant role in economy	Government may have a significant role in economy	State-controlled economy
Unemployment determined by combination of the free market and government policy	Unemployment determined by combination of the free market and government policy	Officially no unemployment
May have religious freedom	Religious worship limited to the state religion	No freedom of religion
Civil liberties and civil rights may be curtailed by government, especially economic rights; widespread social welfare programs (such as free education, health care, and housing)	Limited or no civil liberties or civil rights; social welfare programs are limited	Limited or no civil liberties or civil rights; widespread social welfare programs (such as free education and health care)

DEMOCRACY	DICTATORSHIP	MONARCHY*
Multiple legal political parties	Often only one legal political party	May have no legal political parties, or only one
Free rule by the people through elections	Limited or no electoral freedom; rule by a single individual	Limited or no electoral freedom; rule by a single individual; monarchy may be hereditary or elective
Opposition and dissent are accepted and may be encouraged	Opposition and dissent are limited or forbidden	Opposition and dissent may be limited or forbidden
Private property protected by law and constitution	Limited property rights	Limited property rights, usually inherited; monarch may claim ownership of entire kingdom
Economy determined by free market	Government may have significant role in economy	Government may have significant role in economy
Unemployment determined mainly by the free market	Unemployment determined by combination of the free market and government policy	Monarch may determine how people are to be employed; forced labor may be required
Freedom of religion	Some religious freedom, if it does not threaten the regime	Religious freedom may be allowed if it does not threaten the regime, or not, depending on ruler
Widespread and comprehensive civil liberties and civil rights; some social welfare	Limited or no civil liberties and civil rights; social welfare programs are limited	Social welfare programs may be limited

*Monarchy here refers to absolute monarchy, the traditional form of monarchy known in many earlier kingdoms but rare today; modern constitutional monarchies are monarchies in name only and are typically governed by democratic or socialist republics.

Timeline

c. 365 BCE
Plato's *Republic* completed

1516
Sir Thomas More's *Utopia* completed

1625–1649
English Civil War

1762
Rousseau's *Social Contract* published

1789–1799
French Revolution

1796
Gracchus Babeuf executed May 28

1826–1828
Robert Owen's New Harmony Colony in Indiana

1841
Brook Farm, a Transcendentalist phalansterie

1847
Marx's and Engels's *Communist Manifesto*

1848
Year of revolutions

1867
Karl Marx's *Capital*, the "Socialist Bible"

1884
Engels' *The Origins of Private Property, the Family, and the State*
Fabian Society founded

1889
Second International

1910–1917
Mexican Revolution

1917
Russian Revolution breaks out

1918
U.S. Socialist Eugene V. Debs sent to prison

1919
German Social Democrats head coalition government
Emiliano Zapata, Mexican revolutionary, murdered

1924
Ramsay McDonald becomes British Member of Parliament

1928
Norman Thomas, Socialist Party candidate for U.S. presidency

1933
U.S. Congress authorizes Tennessee Valley Authority

1937
Death of Antonio Gramsci

1938
Mexican president nationalizes foreign oil interests

1940
Trotsky murdered in Mexico on Stalin's orders

1945
Clement Atlee becomes British prime minister after
Labour Party landslide

1948
Yugoslavia expelled from Cominform

1972
United Tasmania Group (first Green Party) founded

1971
Switzerland grants women right to vote

1974
Friedrich Hayek and Gunnar Myrdal share Nobel Prize in Economics

1976
Swedish filmmaker Ingmar Bergman arrested for tax evasion

1979
British Prime Minister Margaret Thatcher begins to
dismantle socialism

1980
Death of Josip Broz "Tito"

1982
Alva Myrdal wins Nobel Peace Prize

1991
Death of Milovan Djilas

Notes

Introduction

p. 9, par. 1, The most widely read, though hardly the most objective history of socialism is probably Harry W. Laidler's *The History of Socialism: A Comparative Survey of Socialism Communism, Trade Unionism. Cooperation, Utopianism, and Other Systems of Reform, and Reconstruction* (New York: Thomas Crowell, 1968).

p. 10, par. 3, An extensive treatment of the Soviet Union and Eastern Europe, which are covered by a volume on communism in this series, has not been included.

p. 11, par. 3, For general treatments of liberalism, *see* Arblaster, Anthony. *The Rise and Decline of Western Liberalism.* (Oxford: Basil Blackwell, 1987), and John Gray, *Liberalism* (Minneapolis: University of Minnesota Press, 1986).

p. 11, par. 4, For the evolution of conservative movements in the United States, *see* Paul Gottfried and Thomas Fleming, *The Conservative Movement* (Boston: Twayne/Macmillan, 1981).

Chapter 1

p. 15, par. 2, N. Lenin was the party name of Vladimir Ilyich Ulyanov. The "N." stands for nothing.

p. 15, par. 3, For working definitions of socialism, capitalism, and communism, *see* the *Oxford English Dictionary*, and Roger Scruton, *A Dictionary of Political Thought* (New York: Hill and Wang, 1982).

p. 17, par. 1, For a history of the utopian tradition, *see* Frank E. and Fritzie P. Manuel, *Utopian Thought in the Western World* (Cambridge, MA: Harvard University Press, 1979).

p. 18, par. 3, Garret Hardin, "The Tragedy of the Commons," *Science*, 162 (1968):1243–1248.

p. 20, par. 1, Many of these groups of "free spirits" have been demonized by conservatives and praised by Marxists as advocates of communism, theft, and free love, but much of the information against them comes from confessions produced under torture or from the reports of enemies and informers. See *The Heresy of the Free Spirit in the Later Middle Ages*. Robert E. Lerner (Berkeley: University of California Press, 1972).

p. 20, par. 2, Acts 5:34–35.

p. 20, par. 5, Genesis 4:19.

p. 23, par. 3, Texts of More's *Utopia* and other utopian writings are collected in *Ideal Commonwealths*, edited by Henry Morley (reprinted Port Washington, NY: Kennikat Press, 1962).

p. 24, par. 2, *The New Atlantis* was written in the 1620s and only published in 1627, a year after Bacon's death.

p. 24, par. 2, The Rosicrucians were a fictional brotherhood of mystics described in a series of pamphlets. Although there were no Rosicrucians, many serious people, including the philosopher René Descartes, believed in their existence.

Chapter 2

p. 29, par. 1, John Gay, *The Enlightenment: An Interpretation*, Vol. II: *The Science of Freedom* (New York: Norton, 1968, pp. 194–201).

p. 30, par. 3, For the revolutionary tradition, *see* James Billington, *Fire in the Minds of Men: Origins of the Revolutionary Faith*. (New York: Basic Books, 1980).

p. 32, par. 1, The manifesto was written not by Babeuf but by his friend Sylvain Maréchal.

p. 34, par. 1, Robert Nisbet, *The Sociological Tradition*. (New York: Basic Books, 1966).

p. 37, par. 4, This principle has been institutionalized by the Supreme Court ruling in the case of *Kelo* v. *New London*.

p. 38, par. 1, 1848 was a year of revolutionary violence in Poland, Germany, France, Italy, and the Hapsburg Empire—in Austria, Hungary, Bohemia, and the Balkans.

p. 44, par. 2, Ruskin was a prominent essayist and art critic of Victorian England. He did much to popularize the Middle Ages.

p. 44, par. 2, For a libertarian critique of Guild Socialism, *see* Ludwig von Mises, *Socialism: An Economic and Sociological Analysis*. Tr. J. Kahane (Indianapolis: Liberty Classics, 1981, pp. 229-232).

p. 47, par. 2, James Burnham, *The Machiavellians: Defenders of Freedom* (Washington, DC: Regnery/Gateway, 1987).

p. 47, par. 2, By Rudy Dutschke, a radical German student leader of the late 1960s.

p. 47, par. 2–p. 48, par. 1, Zoltan Tar, *The Frankfurt School: The Critical Theories of Max Horkheimer and Theodor W. Adorno* (New York: Schochen, 1985).

p. 48, par. 1, The Frankfurt School approach took many forms, some of them conservative, as in the case of the late Paul Piccone, editor of the journal *Telos*, which made important contributions to the study of right-wing and populist political movements.

p. 48, par. 1, The source is Engels, who reported the story on several occasions, cf. the discussion of context in Alex Callinicos, *The Revolutionary Ideas of Karl Marx*. 2nd ed. (London & Sydney: Bookmarks, 1995, p.11).

Chapter 3
p. 50, par. 2, Translated documents from the Second International can be found at http://www.Marxists.org

p. 52, par. 4, The most respected academic history of modern socialism is Donald Sasson's *One Hundred Years of Socialism*, cf. 120–121.

p. 53, par. 4, Enrique Krauze, *Mexico, Biography of Power: A History of Modern Mexico, 1810–1996*. Tr. Hank Heifetz (New York: Harper, 1997, 360).

p. 56, par. 2, The Spanish conquest of South America vastly increased the supply and thus lowered the value of gold in Europe.

p. 67, par. 3, Graham Hancock. *Lords of Poverty: The Power, Prestige, and Corruption of the International Aid Business*. New York, Atlantic Monthly Press, 1989.

p. 68, par. 4, This argument, first applied within nations by John Rawls, in *A Theory of Justice* (Cambridge, MA: Harvard University Press, 1971), has been extended to cover international relations by, for example, Charles R. Beitz in *Political Theory of International Relations* (Princeton: Princton University Press, 1979).

Chapter 4

p. 73, par. 3, Assar Lindbeck, "Swedish Lessons for Post-Socialist Countries," Institute for International Economic Studies (Stockholm), Seminar Paper 645, August 1998, p. 9.

p. 74, par. 2, Article 1, section 9: "No Capitation, or other direct, Tax shall be laid, unless in Proportion to the Census or Enumeration herein before directed to be taken."

p. 77, par. 3, For a highly critical account of Roosevelt and the New Deal by a prominent contemporary, *see* John T. Flynn, *The Roosevelt Myth: A Critical Account of the New Deal and Its Creator* (New York: Devin Adair, 1948).

p. 78, par. 2, In 1920 Charles Ponzi set up a scheme that promised to pay investors 50 percent per month by investing their money in postal coupons used for international transactions. In fact, there were no profits, and Ponzi used his growing pool of suckers to pay the interest he owed to earlier investors. After a dizzying ride to the wealth and fame, Ponzi crashed into bankruptcy and served three and a half years of a five-year sentence.

p. 80, par. 3, For a moderate assessment of Dutch euthanasia, *see* the report of an International Task Force: http://www.internationaltask force.org/fctholl.htm

p. 81, par. 1, Christopher Jenks. *Inequality: A Reassessment of the Effect of Family and Schooling in America.* New York: Basic Books, 1972.

p. 82, par. 3, Kollontai's writings and a biography are available at http://www.marxists.org/archive/kollonta/index.htm

p. 83, par. 2, Joseph Schumpeter, in *Capitalism, Socialism, and Democracy,* 3rd edition (New York: Harper & Row, 1950), showed how capitalism undermined the bourgeois family and set women free from families to become employees.

p. 83, par. 3, cf. Chapter III, p. [16].

p. 83, par. 4, For the Swedish experiment, *see* Allan Carlson, *The Swedish Experiment in Family Politics* (New Brunswick, NJ: Transaction, 1990), and "The De-Institutionalization of Marriage: The Case of Sweden," *The Family in America*, (20) February/March 2006.

p. 86, par. 4–p. 87, par. 1, Mary Ann Glendon, *Abortion and Divorce in Western Law* (Cambridge, MA: Harvard University Press; 1987).

p. 88, par. 1, Peter Stein, "Sweden: From Capitalist Success to Welfare State Sclerosis," *Cato Policy Analysis* No. 160, Sept. 10, 1991.

p. 88, par. 2, "The budget for 2005: a commitment to more jobs and increased welfare." Swedish Ministry of Finance September 20, 2004. http://www.sweden.gov

p. 88, par. 2, "Nation holds OECD income tax record," *Copenhagen Post On Line*, 10.21.04.

Chapter 5

p. 90, par. 1, Thomas Molnar. *Utopia: The Perennial Heresy*, p. 83.

p. 94, par. 2, For the evolution of the Bill of Rights, *see* Akhil Reed Amar. *The Bill of Rights: Creation and Reconstruction* (New Haven, CT: Yale University Press, 1998).

p. 95, par. 4, For evidence on Marx's racism and anti-Semitism, *see* Nathaniel Weyl, *Karl Marx Racist* (New Rochelle, NY: Arlington House, 1979).

p. 98, par. 3, Chicano is a common term used to describe Mexican Americans.

p. 98, par. 3, For a sampling, *see* Chon A. Noriega and others, eds. *The Chicano Studies Reader, 1976-2000: An Anthology of Aztlan* and F. Arturo Rosales, *Chicano! The History of the Mexican American Civil Rights Movement* (Houston: Arte Publico Press, 1997).

p. 100, par. 3, Hayek, *The Servile State*, 241.

p. 100, par. 4, The classic case for international equality was made by Barbara Ward. *The Rich Nations and the Poor Nations* (New York: Norton, 1962).

p. 100, par. 4–p. 101, par. 1, For international aid and its problems, *see* Thomas Fleming, *The Morality of Everyday Life*, chapter 3.

p. 101, par. 1, François Hincker, "The French Socialists," in *Looking Left*, 114.

p. 101, par. 3, P. T. Bauer, *Equality, the Third World and Economic Delusion* (Cambridge, MA: Harvard University Press, 1982).

p. 102, par. 1, Donald Sasson, *One Hundred Years*, 678.

p. 104, par. 1, For a philosophical critique of Marxist theories of exploitation, *see* David Gordon, *Resurrecting Marx: The Analytical*

Marxists on Freedom, Exploitation, and Justice (New Brunswick, NJ: Transaction Books, 1990).

Chapter 6

p. 106, par. 2, Aristotle's criticisms of his teacher Plato can be found in many of his works, especially *Nicomachean Ethics* and *Politics*.

p. 106, par. 4, *The Doctrine of Saint-Simon: An Exposition, First Year, 1828-29* 2nd ed. Tr. by George G. Iggers (New York: Schochen, 1972).

p. 107, par. 3, On Public Choice Theory, *see* James Buchanan and Gordon Tullock, *The Calculus of Consent: Logical Foundations of Constitutional Democracy* (Ann Arbor: University of Michigan, 1965); and applied to bureaucracy, G. Tullock, *The Politics of Bureaucracy* (Washington: Public Affairs Press, 1965).

p. 108, par. 1, C. Northcote Parkinson, *Parkinson's Law* (London: John Murray, 1958).

p. 108, par. 2, *The Limits of Pure Democracy*. Repr. Transaction, cf. Russell Kirk, *The Conservative Mind*, 407–408.

p. 110, par. 2, Juvenal, *Satires* VI, ll. 347–348.

p. 112, par. 4, Joseph A. Schumpeter, *Capitalism, Socialism, and Democracy*, 3rd edition (New York: Harper & Row, 1950), especially ch. 16, "The Civilization of Capitalism."

p. 113, par. 3, Hayek, *The Road to Serfdom*, 55.

p. 113, par. 3, op. cit., 55.

p. 115, pars. 3–4, Hilaire Belloc, *The Servile State*, with introduction by Robert Nisbet. (Indianapolis: Liberty Classics, 1977), reprint of 1913, especially sections 8 and 9. In his introduction, Robert Nisbet, a great political sociologist, recalls that as a young man infatuated with the New Deal, he realized that Belloc had anticipated FDR's revolution by twenty years.

p. 116, par. 1, *I'll Take My Stand* by Twelve Southerners (Baton Rouge: Louisiana State University Press, 2006), and Herbert Agar, ed. *Who Owns America: A New Declaration of Independence* (Wilmington, DE: ISI Books, 1999).

p. 116, par. 4–p. 117, par. 1, James Burnham, *The Managerial Revolution*.

p. 117, par. 2, Ortega y Gasset, *Revolt of the Masses* (New York: Norton, 1994).

p. 117, par. 3, Gabriel Marcel. *Man Against Mass Society*. Tr. G. S. Fraser (Chicago: Regnery, 1952).

p. 117, par. 4, For Bernstein, a German socialist leader, *see* chapter II, p. [16].

p. 118, par. 4, Milton and Rose Friedman, *Free to Choose: A Personal Statement* (New York: Harcourt, 1990).

p. 118, par. 4–p. 119, par. 1, Ludwig von Mises, *Socialism*, p. 264.

Further Information

Books

Carlson, Allan. *The Swedish Experiment in Family Politics*. New Brunswick, NJ: Transaction, 1990.

Engels, Friedrich. *The Origins of the Family, State, and Private Property*. Honolulu: University Press of the Pacific, 2001.

Marx, Karl, and Friedrich Engels. *The Communist Manifesto*. G. C. Jones, ed. London: Penguin, 2002.

Sasson, Donald. *One Hundred Years of Socialism: The West European Left in the Twentieth Century*. New York: The New Press, 1996.

Web Sites

Encyclopedia of British History: Socialism.
http://www.spartacus.schoolnet.co.uk/socialism.htm

Internet Modern History Sourcebook: Socialism.
http://www.fordham.edu/halsall/mod/modsbook33.html

Marxism.org
http://www.marxism.org/

Socialist History Project: Documenting the revolutionary socialist tradition in Canada.
http://www.socialisthistory.ca

Bibliography

Agar, Herbert, ed. *Who Owns America: A New Declaration of Independence.* Wilmington, DE: ISI Books, 1999.

Bauer, P. T. *Equality, the Third World and Economic Delusion.* Cambridge, MA: Harvard University Press, 1982.

Belloc, Hilaire. *The Servile State,* with introduction by Robert Nisbet. Indianapolis: Liberty Classics, 1977, repr. of 1913.

Billington, James H. *Fire in the Minds of Men: Origins of the Revolu-tionary Faith.* New York: Basic Books, 1980.

Brandt, Willy, ed. *North-South: A Programme for Survival.* Cambridge, MA: MIT Press, 1980.

Burnham, James. *The Managerial Revolution.* Westport, CT: Greenwood Press, 1972.

_____. *The Machiavellians: Defenders of Freedom.* Washington, DC: Regnery/ Gateway, 1987.

Carlson, Allan. *The Swedish Experiment in Family Politics.* New Brunswick, NJ: Transaction, 1990.

_____. "The De-Institutionalization of Marriage: The Case of Sweden," *The Family in America,* (20) February/March 2006.

Djilas, Milovan. *The New Class: An Analysis of the Communist System.* New York: Praeger, 1957.

Engels, Friedrich. *The Origins of the Family, State, and Private Property.* Honolulu: University Press of the Pacific, 2001.

Fleming, Thomas. *The Morality of Everyday Life.* Columbia, MO: University of Missouri Press, 2004.

Friedman, Milton and Rose. *Free to Choose: A Personal Statement.* New York: Harcourt, 1990.

Gedicks, Al. *Resource Rebels: Native Challenges to Mining and Oil Corporations.* Cambridge, MA: South End Press, 2001.

Glendon, Mary Ann. *Abortion and Divorce in Western Law*. Cambridge, MA: Harvard University Press, 1987.

Gordon, David. *Resurrecting Marx: The Analytical Marxists on Freedom, Exploitation, and Justice*. New Brunswick, NJ: Transaction Books, 1990.

Gottfried, Paul, and Thomas Fleming. *The Conservative Movement*. Boston: Twayne/Macmillan, 1981.

Hancock, Graham. *Lords of Poverty: The Power, Prestige, and Corrup-tion of the International Aid Business*. New York: Atlantic Monthly Press, 1989.

Ingle, Stephen. *The British Party System*. Oxford, UK: Blackwell, 1987.

Jenks, Christopher. *Inequality: A Reassessment of the Effect of Family and Schooling in America*. New York: Basic Books, 1972.

Kirk, Russell. *The Conservative Mind from Burke to Eliot*. 7th ed. Washington, DC: Regnery, 1986.

Krauze, Enrique. *Mexico, Biography of Power: A History of Modern Mexico, 1810–1996*. Tr. Hank Heifetz. New York: Harper, 1997.

Laidler, Harry W. *The History of Socialism: A Comparative Survey of Socialism, Communism, Trade Unionism, Cooperation, Utopianism, and Other Systems of Reform and Reconstruction*. New York: Thomas Crowell, 1968.

Lampe, John R. *Yugoslavia as History: Twice There was a Country*. 2nd ed. Cambridge: Cambridge University Press, 2000.

Mallock, W. H. *A Critical Examination of Socialism*, London, New York: Harper, 1907.

Marx, Karl. *Capital*, Vols. I & II, London: Penguin, 1992–1993.

Marx, Karl, and Friedrich Engels. *The Communist Manifesto*. G. C. Jones, ed. London: Penguin, 2002.

Mises, Ludwig von. *Socialism: An Economic and Sociological Analysis*. Tr. J. Kahane. Indianapolis: Liberty Classics, 1981.

Noriega, Chon A. and others, ed. *The Chicano Studies Reader, 1976–2000: An Anthology of Aztlan*. Los Angeles: UCLA Chicano Studies Research Center, 2001.

Ortega y Gasset, Jose. *The Revolt of the Masses*. New York: Norton, 1994.

Parkinson, Northcote. *Left Luggage: A Caustic History of British Socialism from Marx to Wilson*. New York: Houghton Mifflin, 1967.

Roepke, Wilhelm. *The Social Crisis of Our Time*. repr. from 1942 ed. New Brunswick, NJ: Transaction, 1992.

Rosales, F. Arturo. *Chicano! The History of the Mexican American Civil Rights Movement*. Houston: Arte Publico Press, 1997.

Sasson, Donald. *One Hundred Years of Socialism: The West European Left in the Twentieth Century*. New York: The New Press, 1996.

Sasson, Donald, ed. *Looking Left: Socialism in Europe after the Cold War*. New York: The New Press, 1997.

Scruton, Roger. *A Dictionary of Political Thought*. New York: Hill and Wang, 1982.

Shaw, George Bernard. *The Intelligent Woman's Guide to Socialism, Capitalism, Sovietism, and Fascism*. London: Constable, 1928.

Stein, Peter. "Sweden: From Capitalist Success to Welfare State Sclerosis," *Cato Policy Analysis* No. 160, Sept. 10, 1991.

Tar, Zoltan. *The Frankfurt School: The Critical Theories of Max Horkheimer and Theodor W. Adorno*. NY: Schochen, 1985.

Twelve Southerners. *I'll Take My Stand*. Baton Rouge: Louisiana State University Press, 2006.

Weyl, Nathaniel. *Karl Marx, Racist*. New Rochelle, NY: Arlington House, 1979.

Index

Page numbers in boldface are illustrations, maps, and charts.

About the Author

Thomas Fleming is the author of *The Morality of Every-day Life*, *The Politics of Human Nature*, *Montenegro: the Divided Land*, and coauthor of *The Conservative Movement*. He holds a Ph.D. in classics and has contributed to newspapers, magazines, and academic journals in the United States and Europe. *Socialism* is his first book for Marshall Cavendish Benchmark.